DEDICATION

To my Mom and Guillermo, thank you for your love and support.
I couldn't do this without you.

To my Dad and Brother, I miss you and love you,
I hope I make you both proud.

To my family, friends and supporters: Thank you for everything.
You're the ones that make me work harder.
I appreciate you more than you can imagine.

I WISH I KNEW:

Lessons in Entrepreneurship I Learned the Hard Way
(So You Don't Have To)

I WISH I KNEW:

Lessons in Entrepreneurship I Learned the Hard Way
(So You Don't Have To)

ANTHONY CHAPTAL TAYLOR

Contents

INTRODUCTION:

YOU DON'T KNOW WHAT YOU DON'T KNOW

You have to be crazy to be reading this book. You really do.

If you're thinking about starting your own business or you already have a business of your own, then you must be crazy. And I mean that in the nicest possible way.

The reports can vary considerably, depending on who you ask, but Bloomberg says that some 8 out of 10 entrepreneurs fail within their first 18 months of business. Other reports have indicated that 50 percent of new businesses fail in the first year and as much as 95 percent fail within the first five years.

Even if we take the more optimistic viewpoint that "only" 50 percent of businesses fail to survive through their first five years, it's clear enough that the odds are stacked against you. Statistically, you're not very likely to succeed in the short term and even less likely in the long term.

After all this time, you would think by now that there would be some sort of "recipe for success" that everyone could reference in order to forge their own path to riches and accomplishments.

Spoiler alert: It's not in this book. In fact, you're not going to find it in any book.

That's because it simply does not exist. There is no single recipe that's going to work for all entrepreneurs and small business owners all of the time under all possible circumstances. There is no one formula, because every person is going to interpret the so-called recipe in very different ways. The recipe needs to be and is made for different people facing different circumstances. And let's not forget that some people just don't follow instructions very well in the first place.

Yes, that includes most entrepreneurs. Either we're too stubborn or too independently minded for that. Perhaps this is what draws us into starting, owning and running our own businesses in the first place, because we want to do things our own way without having to follow strict instructions or to be told what to do by someone else.

While there is no one recipe or formula for success, those that seek it are all looking for the same thing: more money, more freedom, the ability to leave a legacy, the desire to challenge themselves, or even to change the world. The motivations are many and the paths are even more numerous.

We all go off on our own journeys, using the ingredients and tools that we have at our disposal. We set out on this bold endeavor to try and make recipes that will produce the dishes that we want to have.

The problem is that most of us just aren't very good cooks, so we keep trying all sorts of different recipes using all sorts of ingredients and tools with the hope that some day, somehow, we make something that starts to taste good. That's progress. And then we keep refining our techniques and our recipes until we get that much closer to the perfect dish. Perfection itself does not exist, but the pursuit of perfection is very real and positively invaluable.

This book is the culmination of my recipes that didn't work. I wrote this book to try and save you both time and money on ingredients and equipment. Learn from my failures to help bolster your shot at success.

Meanwhile, I'm going to be in the kitchen for the rest of my days. It's where I belong. It's where I feel at home.

I got started as an entrepreneur because I wanted to be able to create something for my future family. I wanted to create a system for wealth that was bigger than me so that I could spend more time at home. The biggest problem with a traditional job is that you are effectively trading hours for dollars and you've only got so many hours in the day. By creating a system outside of yourself, you can continue to generate income even when you're not actively working.

People ask me how I got started as a business consultant. People ask how I got started as an entrepreneur. I just tell them I made it up. And honestly, I'm still making it up.

Yes, I ran a few businesses before I started my consulting business, so I do know what it's like to run a company of my own. And I do in fact have a business degree, so I know something about how businesses are "supposed to work."

However, most of my business knowledge, most of the things that I've learned about running a successful business were learned by doing, they were learned by trying, and yes, they were learned by failing too.

Don't get me wrong. There are many things that I wish I knew before I got started down this path. They would have saved me so much time, money, stress and, in some cases, even tears. I didn't know then, but I trudged on.

That's the game though.

You never know what's going to come your way in business. There are plenty of people with MBAs (Masters of Business degrees) who fail as entrepreneurs. And then you have people who might not impress you on paper, but they have businesses that impress the best of the best. Education only gets you so far.

My hope is that by the time you get to the end of this book, you would have picked up a few practical tips that will help you in your journey as an entrepreneur, some tips for your business, some tips on how the world affects your business, and some tips for yourself as the entrepreneur and human being.

I've kept this book at such a length that you should be able to finish it in an afternoon of reading, if that's what you want to do. In the process, you will learn some of the toughest lessons that I had to teach myself over the course of my over ten years as an entrepreneur and independent business consultant.

The chapters are purposely short and they touch on almost every area of owning a business. If you want more information about any of the topics written herein, take 20 to 30 minutes and do more research online. In particular, spend some time on the website that accompanies this book, elevatedbusinesslife.com. There, you'll be able to get a stronger grasp on how to use these learning opportunities for your specific situation.

This book is not meant to provide all the answers to all the questions you may have. Instead, this book is meant to plant the seed of an idea, so that it can grow with you over time. Throughout the book, I also recommend other resources that you should use to increase your chances of success as a business owner.

My final recommendation before we get started is to remember why you're doing all this in the first place. Remember, there is no one recipe for success. The recipe isn't really that important in the grand scheme of things. What's important is what you're trying to make.

If you focus on why you're doing what you're doing, you'll find a way how to do it.

So, let's get into it. Grab a pen and a pad of paper, take some notes, and I hope that what I've learned can help you on your way to creating your own recipe for success.

PART 1: YOU AS AN INDIVIDUAL

WHAT DOES IT MEAN TO BE AN ENTREPRENEUR?

As we begin our time together, it's important to frame what it is to be an entrepreneur. You can find endless quotes about the life of an entrepreneur, but the reality of it cannot be quoted; it can only be lived, and more accurately, endured.

Starting a business is an all-encompassing adventure that will impact all areas of your life.

What's great is that no matter who you are or what your circumstances are, you can do it. Man or woman, young or old, wherever you are reading this, whatever you are going through, you can become an entrepreneur, you can run your own business, and you can get in the driver's seat of your own life.

Like everyone else, I've had my life challenges. I've had difficulties that I could have used as excuses for not doing what I wanted. But that's not why I know you can be a successful entrepreneur. It's not because I've done it that I know you can be successful; it's because others have done it that I know you can be successful.

People who should have all the odds stacked against them—poor, mental challenges, family problems, no money, whatever it is—they have done it, and that's how I know that you can too.

There are two key factors that separate the people who make it and the ones who don't:

1. **Work ethic**

2. **Drive**

The ones that make it simply want it more than the ones that don't. They stay the late hours, they study, they learn, they make mistakes, they fall and they get back up.

Having money doesn't make a good business.

Having a great idea doesn't make a good business.

Having luck doesn't make a good business.

Having connections doesn't make a good business.

Having a formal education doesn't make a good business.

All those things combined can help make a good business, sure, but being willing to put in the work to make an idea come to life is what will make a business successful.

Being an entrepreneur means putting the time and work in to bring your idea to life. It means overcoming all those challenges and all those reasons why it won't work. It means finding the one reason why it will work and following that until you are successful.

As we chat together over the following pages, realize that being an entrepreneur is first and foremost about doing the work, and progressively moving forward on an idea until you arrive to success.

As it was once said:

"The opposite of success is not failure. It's quitting."

DON'T COMPARE YOURSELF TO OTHERS, BUT LEARN FROM THEM

Being a successful entrepreneur is about focusing on your own plans and executing on them to achieve your vision.

It's really easy to get down on yourself by looking at other entrepreneurs around you and comparing yourself to them. It's especially discouraging when it appears like they are moving far more quickly than you are and you can't figure out why.

Everyone has his or her own struggles. Just because you see what appears to be success on the outside does not mean that they aren't struggling on the inside. That's not to say you should be happy because others are struggling as well, but understand that life is more than what meets the eye, and that everyone has their challenges.

Even if they don't have challenges like you do, it shouldn't matter if they are more successful than you. Just celebrate them. Celebrate their successes. Celebrate their victories. If they can do it, you can too. Build them up instead of taking them down.

Secondly, remember that not all scorecards are the same.

Money is the easiest measure of success, and in our North American society, we look to the dollar as the measuring stick for most people. However, what's more important to you?

I've heard it described as the five F's:

- Family and Friends

- Finances

- Faith

- Fitness

- Fun

If you have lots of money, but don't have the time or energy to enjoy it, what's the point?

Maybe you have relatively less money and have lots of time for family and fun. Is that a better measure of success?

All business owners are playing the same game, but not everyone is using the same scoreboard. What's right for one person who wants to grow a multi-million dollar international business is not the same for the person that wants to create a passive income source or the one who wants to save for retirement.

Finally, no matter who the businessperson is, you can always learn something from them. It might be what not to do, but you can always learn from them.

Experience is costly. Some of the most celebrated and well-known entrepreneurs became successful by making mistakes and paying for them. By taking the time to learn from experienced business owners, you'll be able to sidestep some of the mistakes they have made on your own path to success.

The only caveat I have is that while learning and studying is great, there is no substitute for work and experience. You can spend hours researching how to write sales letters or how to best prospect customers, but if you don't get out there and make a few mistakes yourself, you will never move your business forward.

"Ignorance on fire is better than knowledge on ice."

Make your own mistakes and celebrate your own wins. I'll guarantee that other people will come your way asking how you did it.

SUCCESS IS A MOVING TARGET

Entrepreneurs are goal-driven people. You can't become a successful businessperson without setting goals for yourself and challenging yourself to get better and be better.

That said, success is a moving target. It's important to both recognize how that will affect your business and how it will affect you as a person.

As a business, your objective should be to set goals in regards to revenue, profitability and other metrics that make you stretch beyond where you are at right now. By nature, those goals will cause you to do things differently than how you did them before.

You'll start changing your business model, adapting to customer preferences, trying different forms of marketing, and more. Your business will get to a new stage and you'll repeat the process as needed.

As an individual, on the other hand, being extremely goal-driven like that can have an adverse effect on your happiness. Keep in mind that all businesses have people behind them, and that while a corporation is viewed as a business, it's the humans that guild them that make the machine work.

The reason that being goal-driven can be detrimental to one's happiness is because every time you get close to achieving a goal, you have to move the marker to keep pushing yourself further.

Which means that you are often never satisfied with where you are. There's always more. There's always higher. There's always bigger and better.

Personally, I found it very challenging to be an entrepreneur. I would get hit with bouts of depression thinking that I wasn't where I wanted to be or that things weren't going the way that I wanted them to go. What helped me was sharing those feelings with an entrepreneur or mentor who encouraged me to look back at where I was one year, two years, three years prior to see just how far I had come.

That perspective helped me realize that I was more successful than I had thought. It's important to take the time to be grateful for your past successes and milestones, while still maintaining the drive and passion that got you there in the first place.

SET **SMART** GOALS

Effective goal setting is an important part of being productive and moving forward on what you're trying to achieve, both in life and in business.

When I work with people and I ask them what they are working towards, or what they are trying to accomplish, they often provide great answers. The problem is that these answers happen to lack a few pieces of information crucial to effective goal setting.

There's a saying by management guru Peter Drucker: "What gets measured, gets managed." Setting SMART goals is a great way to create a mechanism to track your progress effectively. because it gives you a way to measure how far you've come.

So, what does SMART stand for?

- **S**pecific
- **M**easureable
- **A**ctionable
- **R**ealistic
- **T**ime bound

Whether you're tracking revenue you want to earn, sales you want to increase, weight you want to lose, or books you want to read, you can use the SMART formula to track and measure where you are against where you want to go. And you can look back to see how far you've come too.

(You can download our balanced scorecard template to use in your own goal setting at elevatedbusinesslife.com)

Examples of SMART goal setting:

I want to increase my sales.

vs.

I want to increase my sales by $50,000 by March 31st.

Our company is going to decrease the number of returns on our products.

vs.

Our company is going to decrease the returns on our products to under 5%.

Each one of our customers is going to buy more from us during the year.

vs.

We are going to increase per customer sales by $40 per transaction.

The different approach to goal setting will not only help you measure your progress more effectively, but also help you with creating strategies and plans to make the improvements you desire.

MEASURING ACTIVITY OR GOALS:
HOW TO MEASURE AND ADJUST YOUR PROGRESS

Goals are great as a measure of success. They help to keep your energy focused on the task at hand and at the desired final outcome. Once you have the goal in mind, you can then start planning on what you need to do next and how much of it you have to do.

In this chapter, we're going to talk about leading and lagging indicators as a way of tracking your goal progress. In simple terms, this is the difference between adjusting the amount of activity that you do to achieve the goal, compared to changing the target that you set in the first place.

I'm going to start with a relatable non-business example to get us on the same page.

Let's say you are trying to lose weight before a specific date. Let's say that date is six months from today and that you're trying to lose ten pounds. That seems like a very reasonable and attainable goal. It's also a SMART goal, because you've made it measurable and put a timeframe.

So, you weigh yourself today and you decide that in order to achieve your goal, you have to go to the gym twice a week for six months. You decide that you don't need to make any changes to your diet.

You go on this plan for two months and you weigh yourself again. Sadly, nothing has changed. You wonder, "What gives?" And now the fact remains that you're two months behind on your goal.

So, what do you do?

You have the information about your weight, but does that information really help you about changing your plans in the future?

The information that you have is already history; it's in the past as soon as you get it.

As such, it's not a very useful tool to help you adapt your weight loss strategy. At this point, you need look at the information that contributes to moving the needle on the scale as a measure of the progress you are making towards your goal.

In this instance, you need to look at the leading indicators: the activities that will impact the result.

What activities are you doing to get you closer to the goal? What changes do you have to make to your activity in order to lose those ten pounds?

Are you sticking with your two workout days every week?

Are your workouts burning enough calories? Or do you need to increase the intensity of your exercise routine?

Do you need to adjust the calories coming in so that you burn more calories than you consume?

Measuring progress with fitness and weight loss is easy, because the math is simple and predictable. It's all right there in front of you in black and white.

The world of business is different. Unless you've been in business for a while, you might not know the exact conversion rates of prospects to clients. But don't worry. You will learn how to do this later in the book.

Back to the task at hand, what's important to take away here is that you have two types of measures for the results in your business:

1. **Lagging indicators**: Information about your targets and milestones that are historical in nature. These include revenue, customers, sales, website visitors, and so on. They are useful for reporting, but changing them won't have an impact on outcomes.

2. **Leading indicators:** Information about the activity that contributes to the achievement of those lagging indicators. These include sales calls per week, networking events scheduled, blog posts per week, and number of events hosted.

If you increase or decrease the activities in the leading indicators, they will have a direct impact on the lagging indicators that most people base their goals on. It's all connected.

If you're falling behind on some of your goals, maybe it's time to review your activity. Take a look at your leading indicators to see if what you're putting in is enough to get what you want to achieve.

If you're not, maybe it's time to do more. Or maybe it's time to adjust what you're doing to improve the efficiency of your activities.

WORK SMARTER AND HARDER

If you're self employed or running your own business, no one cares how many hours that you put in on a daily or weekly basis. The actual hours worked don't matter all that much.

This is great, because it's exactly what gives you the freedom to do what you want, when you want, where you want. On the other hand, it means that you have to be your own boss and monitor the work that you do on a daily basis. The responsibility falls squarely on your shoulders and no one else.

If you're coming from the traditional employment world, you'll need to change your mindset from one of working long, to one of working smart and hard. Shift from focusing on the time that you spend to the results that you deliver. Think about the output, not the input.

Studies are beginning to show that overworking is actually less productive in the long term, so it's important to manage your energy and your time effectively to produce the best results for you and for your business. Being at work is not the same as getting work done.

It's imperative to find the times where you are most productive, and work within that schedule to produce whatever it is that you're working on. When we talk about productivity, it's literally when you are producing for yourself or your business.

In the previous chapters, we talked about goals and about the activity that is required to produce the desired outcomes. When we talk about working smart, you need to think of the outcomes that you want and the pieces that contribute to that outcome.

Sometimes you might not know all the steps that you need to take to produce your ideal outcome. That's okay.

What you do need to know is that you can spend your time on

activities that will contribute to your final objective. Or you can spend your time on activities that will simply keep you busy, but have no bearing on where you will go in the future.

Focus on working smart and only work on things that will move you closer to where you want to go. Busy is one thing; busy and productive is another.

Don't be busy just for sake of being busy.

WORK-LIFE BALANCE

You'll quickly realize (if you haven't already) that your business life and your personal life will meld together and that the idea of work-life balance does not really exist.

I'm not suggesting that you only work and that you have no personal time. In fact, I'm suggesting quite the opposite. I'm suggesting that your new work life and your personal life will be profoundly intertwined and that your business will start influencing, in a positive way, how you choose to spend your personal time.

In this era of continuous connectivity, social networks and real life networking, you have to adapt your life choices and prioritize what's most important to you. Everyone has the same amount of time in a day, and invariably you will be faced with increasingly difficult choices on how to spend that time.

Do you go out for drinks with friends, do you work on updating those pages on your website or do you go to that networking event?

If you have kids and a spouse, you'll have to work even harder to prioritize and protect time for your family, in addition to time for your friends and for your business.

It gets tough, because there will be times when want to take the night off to spend with your friends, or do something else because it's more fun than spending time on your business. The temptations are endless.

The challenge is being disciplined and learning to say no when it's important to do so.

We talked earlier about focusing your energy on working smart. Finding work-life integration is a vital component to working smart.

My suggestion is that you don't overwork yourself because you'll burn out. And the work that you do put out will be sub-par at best.

On the other hand, if you only work when it's convenient and prioritize fun and family over your business, then you won't make any progress towards your long-term vision either.

Much like how you have to find the right financial investments, you have to invest your time wisely to get the best returns for your social life and your business life.

There's no formula that works for everyone, but one thing is certain: sacrifices will have to be made and the more you can integrate your work life and your personal life, the more satisfaction you'll have overall.

STAY HEALTHY

As important as your computer, smartphone and any other business tools you might have might appear, your health will prove the most important tool to your success.

Especially during startup mode, you'll be tempted to put your head down and work some crazy hours just to get the business operating. You'll give up sleep. You'll give up proper nutrition. You'll give up going to the gym.

Even if you have the money to hire some staff to take care of the business for you, you'll be needed to give direction and to put work in yourself.

If you're already exercising several times a week and eating right, it's important to keep those habits going even as the stress of extra work and responsibilities pile on.

If you're not someone who enjoys fitness and exercise, I would urge you to begin incorporating an exercise routine into your new entrepreneur lifestyle for a few reasons:

1. It will help you reduce stress
2. It will help give you energy
3. It will help you cleanse out parts of your body
4. It will help get your body and mind feeling "like they should"

I've found that if I'm working away on a project and I can't seem to focus, I just need a little time away to reset my mind and take some time away from that activity.

Often when I'm dealing with a problem or challenge, I go for a good workout followed by a steam in the steam room. For me, it's a form of meditation. With my mind clear from not focusing on work for an hour or so, I can approach the problem with much more clarity that helps me get to the bottom of the issue. I'm empowered with renewed vigor.

Aside from productivity, another benefit is longevity.

Running a business will take its toll on you, no doubt, and if you want to keep it going, you need to be in as good condition as possible. Getting sick or getting injured happens, and that can result in you needing to take a day or two off to rest and to get back to normal.

The challenge is that if you are out of commission for a few days, there's no one to fill the orders, work on the website, or do the other parts of your business that need doing. As a business owner, those responsibilities fall squarely and solely on your shoulders.

Unfortunately, there's no one that can cover for you or do the things that you intended on doing, which means that your business is going to slow down a little.

Downtime happens, but staying healthy will minimize the likelihood that you have to take days off due to illness.

Things as simple as eating right, sleeping a recommended amount, exercising regularly and drinking plenty of water are investments you can make in yourself that will return dividends both in your personal life and in your business.

There's a reason why all of the top CEOs incorporate fitness into their busy routines. They have kids, they have billion dollar companies, and they have hectic travel schedules and yet they still make time for exercise, often daily.

Take the time to work on and invest in your body and mind as part of your business strategy. Just like software and machinery, this investment is sure to pay dividends and give you a higher quality of life.

EARN COMPOUND INTEREST ON LEARNING

There's a strong correlation between millionaires and reading books, and there's a big reason for why: Successful people keep learning new perspectives and tools that they can leverage to grow what they are doing.

I'm a firm believer that you can earn compound interest on your learning. If you read a book in your twenties, you can use that knowledge for all the years that follow.

You don't have to read every business book on the planet (I'm glad you're reading this one), but if you can make a habit of reading a certain number of books each year, it will certainly help keep your mind sharp and add tools to your entrepreneur toolbox.

In addition to reading, there are many other ways you can invest in yourself to learn new skills and perspectives

I believe in "just in time learning." This is where you learn things as you need them instead of just trying to learn everything all of the time. You can spend an infinite amount of time learning, but what you should be focused on is doing.

There are always opportunities to learn, even if you're "too busy." Listen to a podcast while you're making breakfast or driving. Watch lectures and TED talks instead of TV sitcoms. Go listen to a speaker at your local chamber of commerce instead of grabbing drinks with your friends.

The learning you can get from people that have been there and done that is invaluable.

Disclaimer: I do watch TV, probably about five hours a week, and that's because we can't be perfect all the time. But making small changes over time, like watching a TED talk or an entrepreneur interview instead of The Big Bang Theory will pay dividends over the long term.

You can also take courses on Coursera.org or Lynda.com, as well as pursue continuing education at your local university or college. Go to a workshop, seminar, or a speaker event. Find these opportunities through Meetup.com or your local chamber of commerce.

If you can take at least one golden nugget from each "learning activity," I believe it's worth the time and energy spent.

IF YOU'RE NOT READY TO CHANGE, YOU'RE NOT READY TO BE AN ENTREPRENEUR

We've already talked about how running a business is going to be hard, because of the mental pressure of the day-to-day activities. Here's one more thing that's going to challenge you: In order to overcome those new challenges, you have to change and adapt.

You don't need to change who you are as a human being, but you will need to change your habits and your routines.

The environment of business is always changing. The world is changing at an increasingly rapid pace. Those who will continue to be successful are the ones who can adapt to the change and thrive in it.

By taking on the challenge of entrepreneurship, you've already committed to doing something different than you've done before. Getting business cards and having a website is the first step, but being a successful business owner takes dedication, commitment and sacrifice.

You'll be forced to learn a whole new set of skills. You'll have to shift your priorities in regards to where you spend you time and with whom you spend it. And hardest of all, you're going to have to put yourself in some rather uncomfortable situations by trying something new. Because it will all be new.

Personally, one of the hardest things is putting myself in a place to be vulnerable: one where I ask a prospect to buy from me. Even after years of selling dozens of different products and services, being in a position to be rejected is hard and one of the things that I enjoy the least.

In fact, there are a handful of "business things" that I don't like doing and that I can't entirely outsource. These are some of the hardest battles I have in my business and they are with myself.

That said, when I push through and finally do the "hard" things that have to be done, when I do the things that are uncomfortable to do that's when I get the best results in my business. You're going to have to face the same challenges and you too will learn that the hard things that force you outside your comfort zone are where you'll find the greatest success and the biggest opportunities for success.

There are going to be things that don't come naturally to you and that you don't want to do, but if you want to be successful and move to a better place in your business, you must do them.

If you only do the same things, you're only going to get the same results. Put yourself in a position to be successful by challenging yourself every day to do something uncomfortable. If you keep pushing yourself and stretch what you think you're capable of doing, I think the results will surprise you.

HABITS

You can find 101 articles about the habits of successful entrepreneurs and they can be super interesting. What's more important are the habits you actually incorporate into your life. These are what will begin to affect your life.

It's very easy to dedicate bursts of energy into something, and then leave it for a while, and then get back to it when you feel like it.

In my experience, consistent effort (even with little things) done consistently will have a great impact and offer tremendous change over the long term compared to these intermittent big bursts of energy.

I look at habits two ways:

1. The bad things that you want to get out of your life
2. The good things that you want to add into your life

Logic would dictate that if you want to do more of one thing, you have to less of another. We assume that it's a zero sum equation.

What I've found to be helpful is to periodically make a list of things that I want more of, and another list of things that I want less of and see how I can adapt my day to day to incorporate these changes into my life.

They say that it takes 21 days to form a habit. Personally, I haven't found that to be necessarily the case, as I fall in and out of habits as time goes on.

Habits stick the best for me when I connect them with some other part of my day.

- Listening to a podcast when I make breakfast
- Free writing when I'm on the train
- Scheduling my next day before I brush my teeth
- Reading before I go to bed

Just like systems in your business can help you create consistency and scale, personal habits can help you stay consistent on the things that bring you the most benefit and decrease the likelihood that you forget about doing them.

IF YOU'RE GOING THE WRONG WAY, IT'S NEVER TOO LATE TO TURN BACK

I've made more mistakes than I wish to admit. Hopefully though, you can learn from some of my mistakes and borrow that learning to avoid some of the costs that I had to pay for. That's why this book exists.

The first lesson that I want to share is that if you're going the wrong way, it's never too late to turn around.

You're going to try a lot of things in your business. Some are going to work, and some aren't. One of the skills you'll develop as an entrepreneur is the ability to recognize when things are working and to realize when things aren't working and that you should cut your losses.

There's a difference between trying something that doesn't work and quitting before you are successful. Unfortunately, there's no way to tell you which of those opportunities is a good one and which one is a dud.

There's a great story in *Think and Grow Rich* about some gold miners who quit before they had struck gold. The tale is that they were just three feet from gold and had they continued, they would have found the success that they were looking for. But they gave up too soon.

There are many stories from famous entrepreneurs, as well as historical figures, who found their greatest success after encountering their greatest failures.

My advice to you is to take some time periodically to review what's working in your business and what's not. I know it's hard, because you have a laundry list of other things to do, but if you take the time to review your plan every few months, it will save you the money that you could have been wasting had you just let it all continue.

Another way is avoid some mistakes is to set a goal for an activity ahead of time. Then, you can give yourself a timeline for that activity for when you decide to stop doing it.

For example: I'm going to spend $1000 advertising in _____ for 6 months. If I don't get at least $1500 in revenue from it, I'm going to stop.

This will help you do two things:

1. Analyze your opportunities more carefully. If I only have $1000 a month to spend, which advertising opportunity is most likely to get me the return that I desire (i.e., $1,500 in six months).

2. Define the specific outcomes that you need to meet in order to continue on that path.

The challenge is that we often rationalize our decisions even if they aren't the best. By taking this step, you have an extra measure in place to help support your decision making before it happens.

And if you're doing the wrong thing, then you can stop and do something else.

FAILURE IS DESTINED TO HAPPEN, BUT IT'S NOT THE END

It has been said that success is moving from failure to failure without loss of enthusiasm.

If you're trying to run a business without experiencing some sort of failure, you're in for a rude awakening.

Here's the good part: Everyone fails, and failure is not the end of the line.

You can look back at the famous successes in history and note that they were all predicated by a string of failures. Or said another way, "not success yet."

There are a lot of ways you can fail that are actually not your fault, per se.

Your product might be too advanced for the market. It might be too costly to make now, whereas advances in technology might make it easier and more economically viable in the not too distant future.

There are also failures that you have to push through because "it's not there yet."

Maybe your product is great but your marketing and message aren't.

Maybe your product is great but you're targeting the wrong people.

Maybe you're getting customers, but you're having a hard time keeping them.

There are lots of possibilities for those maybes, and as such, you have to keep overcoming challenges until you find certainty into what works.

If you have become an entrepreneur, you have already embraced risk-taking to a certain degree. And if you have embraced risk-taking, then you know that sometimes risks don't work out. That's why they are risky.

Successful entrepreneurs take the risks; accept the potential for failure, and work through it, because they know that the success on the other side is worth more than the failures that we used to create it.

Most successful entrepreneurs credit their success in part to having a good mentor to guide them along the way.

A mentor is anyone who has been to where you want to go. They've traveled the path you desire and you listen to them on a regular basis.

I've had a few formalized mentor/mentee relationships. Some have worked out and some less so. I've also had informal mentor relationships with people that I trust and respect that I reach out to in times of need or when I just want to pick their brain about something.

I can't speak highly enough about the power of a good mentor and what having a mentor in your professional life can do for your business.

Getting a mentor is as easy as reaching out to someone you admire and asking them to go for coffee or a meal and explaining that you're new in the business and you were hoping for some guidance. You'd be surprised how many highly successful people are more than happy to help those just starting out.

LinkedIn is a great tool to be able to reach out to people in your own town, because you can look at their experience first to see if you think their path is something you would like to emulate. Or even if you don't want to follow the same path, you may look to someone who has taken a tangentially related path for a different perspective or source of inspiration.

Before you reach out to these people, you must recognize that if someone is worth going to for advice and guidance that they are probably very busy and their time is very valuable. Recognize and appreciate that.

Secondly, it's important to note that many people get paid to give advice in regards to business. They work as professional consultants or advisors, so you must respect what those people do as a profession versus the time they dedicate to helping others pro-bono.

And finally, no one is obliged to help you with your business, so recognize that if you do get a chance to pick someone's brain about their past successes, be respectful and come prepared. Don't take the opportunity for granted.

Odds are that someone helped them when they were just start-ing out, and this is their chance to return the favour. They're paying it forward, just as you should when you become successful too.

So who do you pick as your mentor? Pick as many people as you want!

Since everyone that you meet has had a different experience than you, you stand to learn from all of them. Maybe in the begin-ning stages, you want to learn from someone who owned a busi-ness just like yours. Perfect.

You might also want to learn from someone who has special skills in marketing, someone else who has done business interna-tionally, or someone who you just met at a speaker event and you liked their attitude and outlook.

Being able to learn from others and apply these lessons to one's own situation is a valuable skill to master, and one that's invaluable for entrepreneurs.

Whether you have a formalized mentor/mentee relationship where you meet every few months or weeks, or an informal board of advisors that you reach out to at specific times, having people with more experience than you who you can look to for advice is one of the smartest things you can get as a new business owner.

PART 2: YOUR BUSINESS

GET IT IN WRITING (IT'S PERSONAL AND BUSINESS)

As you build your business, you'll ultimately build relationships with partners, suppliers, employees and other people that work with and support your business.

As these relationships develop (especially in the beginning), you'll want to foster a culture of trust and friendship.

You also want people to like you and you don't want to do anything that might compromise the relationship or push people away from doing business with you.

It's easy to think that making someone sign a contract would put pressure on the relationship before it even starts.

I've thought that way for a long time, and sometimes I just didn't bother with a contract because I trusted the person on the other side of the table. By not having a contract or a written agreement, the door has been opened to confusion and dissatisfaction by one or more parties.

From a business owner's side, having a contract makes it seem like you're more protected in case your client doesn't pay you.

This is true, but just because there's a contract doesn't automatically guarantee that all parties will agree to it. It just means that they know what they are agreeing to and you have proof that shows that is the case.

So while contacts seem like they could harm a potential business relationship by eroding trust of one of the parties, it's actually designed to help both parties by clearly stating the important facts of the business relationship.

This way, each party knows exactly the exact expectations they have of one another, and if you're selling or buying something, you know clearly what you're getting, what you're not getting, and how much it's going to cost, as well as all the other terms and conditions that apply to your business relationship.

I recommend getting a lawyer to draw up your contracts as a specific template, and view it as an investment into your business processes.

Not only does it show that you are serious enough about your business relationship to have a contract written up by a lawyer--which makes the other party take the relationship just as seriously—but it will also save you time because all you have to do is change the names and certain terms in the contract.

Finally, by having a lawyer advise you on your contracts, you'll be able to put in clauses specific to your business that will both help improve the comprehensiveness of your contract and protect you in the unfortunate chance that you have to go to court.

Not having a lawyer create and review a contract for me was the source of one of my biggest financial mistakes. Not only was getting a lawyer to create and review a contract not as expensive as I thought it would be (the next time), but it paled in comparison to the money I lost from a failed venture because of the sub-par contract I wrote myself.

Get a lawyer to protect and maintain your relationships, because it's business and your business is personal.

FINANCING
(YOU'LL SPEND THE MONEY IF YOU HAVE IT)

I've taken loans for my businesses, I've worked different jobs while running a business, and I've consulted with businesses that have received external investment.

Here's a warning: If you have the money, you will spend it. And you might not spend it wisely.

There's a great book called Scarcity by Eldar Shafir that talks about our ability to make decisions. In it, we learn that your brain, when faced with scarcity, will either go into tunnel vision, missing opportunities and only focusing on the scarcity, or will achieve improved focus because you have to make the most with the little that you have.

Have you ever heard the saying, "If you have something that you need done, give it to a busy person"?

That's because when you're busy, you have to be extra efficient to do all the things that you need to get done. Conversely, if you have lots of something, you're inclined to waste it, or at least use it in a less than optimal fashion.

Whether you have 45 minutes or two hours to do the exact same task, it's human nature to use all the time allotted and stretch it out.

The same is true with money. If you have lots of money in your bank, you'll feel no scarcity on how you spend it. You'll be less frugal and possibly make suboptimal decisions.

You know how the last bit of toothpaste in the tube always lasts the longest? It's because when you know you're near the end, you try to make it last as long as possible.

I've built businesses with money and without it. Hands down, I would take the money to help me grow. It's a lot less stressful and you can do more.

Just keep in mind that if you don't have a good strategy in place to spend your investment, you might end up wasting money, wasting time and wasting opportunities along the way.

Bonus: Please don't spend your money on marketing and promotional items until you have a product that people want. You can spend a near infinite amount of money on marketing, but if you spend more money on making a good product, it will multiply the return on all your marketing. So, focus on getting the right product/market fit first. The t-shirts and bumper stickers can be made later.

SHOULD I BOOTSTRAP OR GET A LOAN?

Money can help you do many things, but money won't give you a good product or a good business. What it can do is leverage a good business and make it great more quickly.

I've seen many business ideas in my career. Some are great, some are terrible and some are just average. The ones that I found the most dangerous are the ones that sit in the middle because it's not so obvious where they will end up and what will happen if you add time and money to them. You could be funnelling your resources into a dead end.

If you were starting a business, you would obviously think that you had a good idea on your hands. Otherwise, you wouldn't go forward with growing it in the first place. You might be so passionate about your idea that you'll re-mortgage your house, take on excessive credit card debt or take out a loan out to make it happen.

Unfortunately, I can't stop you from self-funding a bad idea.

I've taken a mortgage loan out to support businesses that I should have let die, so I'm speaking from experience. What I can do is encourage you to do is take a few specific steps before you consider getting a loan or taking on unnecessary financial risk on an idea.

First, you should write a business plan to flesh out the idea fully, outlining possible risks and impacts from uncertainty. Project your financials for at least two years. Yes, they are just projected numbers, but you'll get a better sense of how much money you're going to need ahead of time. You'll also have a better idea if it's worth the money and time investment to move forward.

Second, figure out what you can afford to invest personally. Consider the worst-case scenario and what you can honestly risk losing. Then, see where the difference is between what you have and what you need to start up your idea.

And finally, make the decision whether you want to take out a loan out and give yourself that extra support to get your business off the ground or if you want just to take the assets that you have now and make it work. This is when your ability to realistically forecast is important. If the minimum amount of money you need to start your business is $20,000, don't start it unless you already have that amount of money on hand.

Think of it this way: Imagine that you are going to swim out to an island located 15 miles away from where you are. However, you know that you can only swim 10 miles without taking a break. Once you're in the middle of the ocean, there is no turning back. If you don't make it, you'll drown. Only when you are honestly prepared to swim the full 15 miles should you plunge yourself into the water.

If you decide to bootstrap and find yourself in a crunch (those last five miles), don't be surprised if your bank does not give you a loan. The best time to ask for a loan is when you don't need it. So whether you get financing from friends and family, or from a financial institution, it's better to have access to the money and not need it, then to need it and not be able to get it.

Regardless of whether you bootstrap or get a loan, do your best to predict the expected start-up and cash requirements as part of your business planning process. Have lines of credit or emergency runway cash ready to go to give yourself a reserve for a rainy day. I guarantee it will rain.

DO I NEED A BUSINESS PARTNER?
WHAT SHOULD I LOOK FOR?

As you go through your business planning process, or start looking at growth models, the question of bringing in a partner might enter the realm of possibility.

There are many successful businesses that have a team of founders or co-founders that complement each other and help grow the business.

Having a partnership can help because you have more than one person out there selling and working on advancing the business on a day-to-day basis. Another benefit is that you'll have a wider range of skills and expertise that you can draw from.

The ideal partner is someone whose skills complement your own, filling in the gaps where you might be lacking and vice versa. If you're good at big picture thinking, having a partner who can focus on the details and look at the smaller practical applications of what you're working on can be valuable. This makes for a good cross-section of perspectives.

In tech, there are often technical and non-technical co-founders. The one with the technical skills, like coding, are needed to build a product or a website. The other co-founder might have the personal or soft skills that are required to get traction in the marketplace. The whole is greater than the sum of its parts.

There are certainly many benefits to working with a partner as you get your business going, but I've also seen many challenges and problems arise from them as well.

A common example is striking the balance between work performed and compensation received. If one person does more work--or seems to be doing more work or feels like he's doing more work--he may feel that he deserves to get more money than his partner. After all, why should someone receive the same amount of money if they really are putting in more effort?

Another challenge that might arise has to do with differences in vision and motivation. What happens if, in a few years, one of you wants to go in one direction and the other wants to go in a different direction? What if there are more than two partners and everyone has a different vision in mind?

While it may seem like a small thing to get over at first, long term, if you and your partners/team aren't going in the same direction, you're in for trouble.

There is also the challenge that can arise from a lack of mutual trust. You need to be able to trust your business partners and know that they have your interests in mind as well as theirs. If you're going into "battle" together, you need to know they have your back, just like you have theirs.

Whether you decide to bring on partners as you begin to grow, or start your business as a partnership, I encourage you not to rush into the process. Start with small tests and work together to see how you mesh and if it's going to be a good fit long term.

Establish your values, your vision and your desires early in the process and save yourself a lot of heartache and business grief down the road. If at any point you think the partnership is going in the wrong direction, please address it right away. If you feel like something isn't right, you're probably correct.

Address whatever issues arise as soon as possible, and I promise the pain of having that hard conversation now will be far less than the potentially catastrophic consequences of waiting to have that conversation later on, not only for you, but also for your partners and your business.

DECISION MAKING AND INVESTMENTS:
WHAT IT TAKES TO GET STARTED ARE SUNK COSTS

You've no doubt heard the expression: "It takes money to make money."

You know that you need to invest into your business to help it get off the ground and turn into more money in the future.

But then, there's also this expression: "Don't throw good money after bad."

That's what I did in one of my last businesses. Instead of taking a loss and letting a failure be what it was, I put more money after it to try and salvage what was there and recoup my initial investment.

As you read that, it doesn't make much sense, does it?

This is the peril of being so close to something that you don't think clearly and objectively.

Why I include that story in this chapter is because while it does take money to get started in a business, and it does take an initial investment, that investment is most likely gone no matter what. It shouldn't guide your decision making in the future and moving forward. That's why they are called sunk costs. (See the last appendix for a full definition.)

When making decisions in your business, take each individual investment and rate of return into consideration. However, make those decisions independently so that previous decisions don't cloud your ability to make good decisions in the future.

The investments you made in the past are gone, so don't make another mistake by trying to fix something you can't do anything about.

MEASURE YOUR INVESTMENTS AND ACTIVITIES

Measuring your ROI, or return on investment, is paramount to having a successful business long term. Getting a return on your investment means getting more out than you put in.

While large organizations measure their ROI in strictly financial terms, it's important as a small business to measure your other resources of time and energy, as well as money. Particularly if you're a solopreneur, you have to be very deliberate with what activities you engage in and what you're hoping to get out of them.

Sometimes you don't know if a networking event or a speaker session will be valuable. You don't know if those flyers are going to have the effect you desire, or if that online marketing is going to attract you new clients right away. But that's why you need to test, track and measure the outcome.

Over time, you'll figure out what works for you and your business. What's worth your time, and what's not. You'll learn where you should focus your energy and where you should pass up "opportunities."

No matter where you are at with your business, before you make an investment into your business, determine what you're hoping to get out of it.

Maybe you decide that you need a 25-50% ROI on your marketing before do anything. The challenge is that you have no idea how it's going to work out. The element of risk is certainly still there.

One other thing to note: just because it didn't turn into something desirable right away does not mean it didn't work.

I landed one of my biggest clients in my fourth year of business from two sources of marketing--search engine optimization and a chamber of commerce--that otherwise had not met that ROI threshold in the short term.

I chose those marketing channels because I believed they would pay off in the long run. They did and I can now share the success story. I also have many investments that didn't prove quite so valuable. Sometimes, it really is a guessing game.

What's important to remember is that you need to get something out of everything you do, whether it's tangible or intangible, whether the benefits come out in the short term, the medium term or in the long term.

Aim to get the largest ROI on your activities because you can't do everything.

MAKING STRATEGIC TRADEOFFS TOWARDS ACHIEVING YOUR VISION

My consulting firm, SME Strategy, helps organizations define their strategies. What is a strategy?

It's what not to do.

That might seem counter-intuitive, but think of all the possible directions you could take with your business: Different customers, different marketing channels, and different business models ... the opportunities are endless.

And therein lies the challenge: There are too many things that you could do, so you need to pick more of the things that will get you closer to where you want to go and less of the things that move you away from where you want to go.

We talked earlier about setting goals and targets for what success looks like. Otherwise known as your business vision, what does the future look like if you're 100% successful?

Just like we talked about getting a positive ROI from your investments, you need to pick investments and activities that will move you closer to where you want to go and where you want to be in the future.

Ask yourself these questions when evaluating choices for your business:

Will this move me closer to my vision of where I see myself at [date]?

Will this help me move forward on my smaller business goals?

Entrepreneurs often are affected by shiny object syndrome. They move from thing to thing that attracts their attention. They get distracted by the new things that might seem like more fun or less difficult, diverting resources and attention away from what they are working on currently.

What happens is by shifting over to a new project, they end up stalling what they were working on before. By shifting to a new project, they often are not helping themselves accomplish their vision.

You can't do everything, so you need to make tradeoffs and choices to pick the things are going to be the most effective at moving you closer to your vision.

If you don't have a vision, if you don't have something that you are aiming at, then you risk wasting time and wasting money because there's nothing focusing your energy towards accomplishing. You're being busy for the sake of being busy.

Once you have your goal, once you have your vision, pick things that are going to move you closer towards those goals and visions, instead of distracting you away from them.

DO I NEED A BUSINESS PLAN?

Clients come to me often asking me to write a business plan for them. In my opinion there are two main reasons you should get a business plan made:

1. To apply for financing

2. To figure out where to take your business and to ask yourself essential questions about your business

Of the four businesses that I've started personally, I've only written one full business plan and I used it to apply for a small operating line of credit.

I would have gone through informal business planning and back of the napkin strategy for some of my other businesses, but I do wish I had gone more into the process for all my businesses.

Here's my number one reason you need a business plan:

You need to be able to answer the questions in the business plan to help you figure out how you're going to run your business.

Download a business plan questionnaire and template at elevatedbusinesslife.com to get started.

My one trepidation with a business plan is that once you write it, all the information is historical in nature. After you've written about your products or services, you might change what you offer, the pricing, or whatever else. Your competitors and your environment will change very quickly.

That's why I'm hesitant for you to spend so much time on a plan, only to leave it on a shelf to be neglected and forgotten.

That said, if you don't take the time to look at your competition, you won't know how you're different or better. You won't know why a customer should choose you over the other guy.

If you don't plan out your costs two years in advance, you might realize that you need more money than you expected to get you businesses off the ground. You'll suddenly be stuck in a rather uncomfortable position.

As I mentioned earlier "If you can only swim 10km, don't begin a trip to an island 15km away."

You need to think of who your customer is, what they care about, and how you're going to reach them as part of your marketing plan.

And much more...

If you want to increase your chances of being successful in your business, write a business plan, or go through the process of having someone write one with you.

Not only will you answer critical questions in order to move your business forward, but it's also a way to minimize the risk on your investment and determine if your business will be profitable and worth the time and money you're going to put into starting it.

DO LESS, DO MORE

There's an expression that I like from the popular TV show *Parks and Recreation*:

"Don't half-ass two things. Whole-ass one thing."

In other words, don't do many things poorly, do one thing well and to completion.

I've seen many entrepreneurs (myself included) get distracted by new projects or opportunities that catch our attention and interest. The end result is that previous projects are left to sit dormant and only partially completed.

I've found it's because it's hard going that final leg when you're already exhausted and maybe even too bored (as what easily happens with entrepreneurs) to finish the last piece of what you're working on.

I've also found it challenging to successfully manage the energy for various projects because of the energy cost of "context switching" from task to task. Each time you switch activities, you waste energy in the process.

Think of it this way: Each activity you do, or each project you work on, is on a different floor of a building. Each time you switch tasks or projects, you have to take the stairs or elevator to get to another floor. If you didn't spend that extra time moving from floor to floor, you would have extra time and energy to spend on that one task.

If you want to be a successful entrepreneur, managing your energy is the key to being effective, moving forward and tackling your to-do list.

To think of it another way, look at the total amount of energy that you have at 100 percent. And the more different tasks that you try to do take different amounts of energy. If you try to do four different things, you'll have a maximum of 25% for each activity. If you focused on only one activity, by contrast, you would have four times more energy to direct to that one activity to move it significantly forward.

WHAT GETS MEASURED GETS MANAGED

Famous strategist Michael Porter said, "What gets measured, gets managed."

If there's an area of your business that you are trying to improve, you have to figure out a way to tangibly measure its progress. Whether you are trying to improve cash flow, improve sales, or any other metric, you can't make improvements unless you know what to look for and how to measure it.

Some people are more detail-oriented than others, and some have more success with self-micro management. One person's style might be best suited to bean counting, whereas another's might be focused on the measurement of the bigger picture.

Regardless of your style, you need to find some kind of accompanying measurements for each of your initiatives.

There's a business methodology called the balanced scorecard that I like to use because it measures more than just profit and revenue. The balance scorecard takes into consideration:

- Financial metrics: Anything that has to do with finances

- Customer metrics: How do we satisfy customer needs?

- Learning and growth: How we improve the people?

- Business processes: How do we make our business processes more efficient?

The great thing about the balanced scorecard is that it's adaptable to all businesses depending on what they want to measure and what they think is the most important.

If you're the owner-operator of your business, you do more than just measure money in and money out. The balanced scorecard will help you measure both your financial and non-financial activities to help you build a well-rounded business.

IT'S NOT WHAT YOU MAKE; IT'S WHAT YOU KEEP

The measure of most successful businesses is financial position, unless you're a non-profit or a mission-based organization (whose objective is to reinvest money and profits to create greater benefit for your stakeholders).

You could also be a for-profit social enterprise that benefits others through their operations, tying community impact and benefit into your business model. In fact, a for-profit business with a social impact portion is my preferred model of business where one of the core values is to share the wealth and to help others.

As famous rapper and entrepreneur Jay-Z once said, "I can't help the poor if I'm one of them. So I got rich and gave back. That's a win-win."

Whether you want to help others with your business or not, you need first to be successful yourself.

How would you measure financial success in revenue or profit?

Many people don't know the difference and use the wrong measures. Revenue is what you bring in. Profit is what you keep. You want to be measuring profit.

Which would you prefer? A business that does one million dollars in revenue and has a net profit of $100,000 or a business that does $200,000 in revenue with $110,000 in net profit?

When building your business focus on what you keep instead of what you make; you'll end up selling the products with higher profit margins and doing relatively less work for more money.

PIECEMEAL IS GOOD, BUT COMPLETE IS BETTER

When starting a business on your own dime, you always have to find ways to make your dollars stretch as far as they can.

Running lean, or Ramen Profitable , is the reality for most startups (unless you get funding, a loan from the bank of mom and dad, or have a severance to draw from). Spending wisely and watching your burn rate are critical to making your business successful long term.

While it's important to be frugal and watch your spending, when looking at investments in infrastructure in your business, think long term. Try to get the best complete package that you can afford.

Technology startups have created amazing and cost effective tools for small and medium businesses to do everything from event management to accounting. They even provide customer management platforms.

(For a list of resources for your business visit elevatedbusinesslife.com/resources.)

When evaluating these options, look at where your business is going to be in a few years to see if that solution will be the best option both in the short and in the medium term of your business.

Picking the least expensive solution that will do the trick now is really like plugging a hole instead of fixing the problem.

What ends up happening is that you spend more money on multiple programs that overlap and take additional inputs on the user side. Moreover, you'll spend time and money changing over data when you do eventually upgrade to that comprehensive solution, the one that fixes the problem versus just patching it up.

The piecemeal solution may seem attractive in the short run, and if you have no other option, do that. But if you can manage the investment of a complete solution from day one, you'll save more money and time overall, and your business will be better for it.

MONEY IS NOT A BAD THING

If you're making money, it means you're offering something people want and are willing to pay for.

Warren Buffett has famously said, "Price is what you pay, and the value is what you get."

Think of the things that you buy in your life. If you think that they're worth the money, you'll buy them. Other times, you look at the price of something and think that it's a rip off and not worth the money. So, you don't buy it.

When you buy something, it's because you're willing to exchange your hard earned money for something that makes your life better. Whether you need it, or just want it, you have the choice to make the purchase.

Now think as a business owner: If you're offering something that people want and see the worth of, then people will pay for it. You're doing a service to the customer by making that product or service available to them.

Conversely, if the product was unavailable or too expensive, then you're not offering any value to the consumer, so it makes sense that they shouldn't pay you for anything. You didn't make their life better. You didn't offer the solution they wanted.

Have you ever seen a product or service that you LOVE, or that made you think, "Where has this been all my life? I wish I knew about this sooner!"

If you're worried about making money or concerned about how your customer is going to view your product, ask yourself if your product or service is helping to improve someone's life. Are you providing value? Are you offering the right solution?

It doesn't have to be life-changing or dramatic; it just needs to be valuable to them in a certain shape or form.

Maybe you're selling products that are hard to find.

Maybe you're giving them a place to hang out and drink coffee that is enjoyable.

Maybe you're giving them confidence or helping them relax.

Whatever it is that you're doing, you're solving some sort of problem or giving them some sort of benefit.

If you don't sell it to them, or rather if you don't allow them to buy it, then you are doing them a disservice. Therefore, if they are giving you money, it's because they want what you're offering and there's nothing wrong with that.

As long as you're not scamming people, or overpromising and under-delivering, then you shouldn't feel bad about getting money for selling a product.

The world gets better because of people like you. Celebrate your ability to offer something that people want, because if you made the money as an entrepreneur, you certainly earned it.

DON'T BUILD YOURSELF A JOB, BUILD A BUSINESS

> GOOD SYSTEMS WILL MAKE YOUR BUSINESS

One of the many reasons that people become entrepreneurs is so that they can experience more freedom and have better control of their time.

Often what ends up happening is that people simply exchange one job for another and trade their time in one area of another.

There's a saying that goes something like "I left my job working eight hours a day for someone else to working sixteen hours a day for myself." In my experience, it's been true.

However, the reasons that you as an entrepreneur put those hours in are to:

- Have control of your time and money
- Gain more financial security
- Earn the sense that you're building something that will keep working when you aren't

In the previous chapter we talked about maintaining good health so that you don't have to worry about missing "work days" in your business due to illness. I want to encourage you to look at your business to see what opportunities exist to create systems and automation in your business so that you haven't built yourself a job. Rather, you want to build a system for making money that operates even when you aren't.

I've heard another entrepreneur say that the only way to make a million dollars is to have your business selling while you sleep.

The best book on the subject of systems is Michael Gerber's *The E-Myth Revisited*.

Get the book. Read it as soon as you can.

Systems in your business will do several things:

- It will make your business more efficient
  (which means less waste of time and money)

- It makes your business safer because it relies less on
  people (and their capacity to remember and do things)

- It makes the business less dependent on you
  (if you're sick or want to take a vacation, or even just
  a day off)

- It allows you to scale, and to grow your business

You only have 24 hours in a day, and if you only rely on yourself, then you truly have built a job, but the business will not be able to grow larger than you. You need systems to transcend that problem.

WHAT'S MORE EXPENSIVE THAN A GOOD ACCOUNTANT OR LAWYER?

Paying for a lawyer and an accountant are two areas where I wouldn't skimp in your business.

Disclaimer: I've had a bad accountant and I've had a great accountant. One got me in a bind and one took me out of one. (It was the same bind that the bad accountant put me in, as you may have already guessed.)

I've tried the do-it-yourself approach for both my legal and accounting needs and I definitely would not recommend it. The only thing more expensive than a good accountant or lawyer is a bad one.

› ACCOUNTANTS

I know many entrepreneurs who want to do their own taxes or go to a large consumer-focused company to get their taxes done in order to save the money that they would have to spend on a dedicated accountant.

In my experience, you'll save more money on your taxes when you work with a dedicated business-oriented accountant, because they will know how to best work with deductions. Not only that, but you'll also get advice that's catered to your future business needs.

Look at your accountant as a partner in the success of your business. This is someone who you plan on working with for several years to come and someone who really has your best interest at heart.

Not only will working with an accountant free up your time to do what you do best in your business, but you'll benefit from their experience in dealing with dozens of other business owners. They'll be able to give you advice that goes beyond where you can find extra deductions, how to minimize tax and how to keep the government at bay.

"He who represents himself has a fool for a client."

Contracts can be expensive. You think to yourself, "Why do I have to spend hundreds of dollars for words on a page when there are dozens of free or cheap templates online?"

Please, for the sake of your future state of mind, and your personal and business financial state of health, at least consult with a lawyer before you get into any significant business agreements.

I was 20 years old when I got into my first major business deal and I did it with a DIY contract template. What I wouldn't give to have that mistake back!

A lawyer can be beneficial for both major business dealings, as well as frequent business transactions.

For my consulting business, I have had contracts drawn up for new hires, new clients, proposals and re-sellers. It was just a one-time expense for each, and now I use the "boilerplate" templates for all my habitual transactions.

The cost was much less that I had originally expected and the fact that I have a contract demonstrates my commitment and seriousness to all of my clients and partners.

UNDERSTANDING YOUR COSTS: FIXED AND VARIABLE

I talk to a lot of people who don't consider themselves "numbers people."

If you're in business for yourself, I suggest you become familiar with numbers and other aspects of finance and bookkeeping. That way, you can better understand and predict what happens with your money on a monthly basis.

Getting a bookkeeper, a tax accountant or a controller to help you with the management of your profits is certainly a good idea when you can afford it. But if you're in the beginning stages of your business, or you are looking to increase your profitability, here is a concept to get into your head.

There are two measures for your costs: fixed and variable.

Fixed Costs and **Variable Costs**.

Fixed Costs are costs that are going to be mostly the same month over month. These costs include such items as your insurance, rent, car loans, other loan payments, cell phone bill, Internet bill, web hosting bill and things that you can predict are going to come out on a regular basis.

Variable Costs are the costs that fluctuate depending on business activity.

For example, if you own a product business, a variable cost would be the cost of your product production before you can sell it for a profit. Your variable costs will vary every month and usually in function with how many products you produce and sell.

If you're a bakery, your flour and sugar costs will go up in busy months and down in slower months, where as rent will stay the same.

The reason you need to understand both fixed and variable costs is that's how you're going to predict where you money is going ahead of time. This way, you don't get into a position where you have limited cash flow.

CASH FLOW IS KING

There are two things that are going to determine the sustainable success of your business: cash flow and retained earnings (money you keep).

You might have lots of accounts receivable (money that's supposed to come in), but if you don't have it when you need it--like when you need to pay your employees--you're going to have to some serious challenges moving forward.

Understanding your cash flow, keeping tabs on your accounts payable (the money that goes out) and your accounts receivable (the money that goes in), will help you manage lots of stress as you grow your business. You don't want to come up short.

There are many stories of entrepreneurs running their businesses off of credit cards and moving money from point A to Point B while in startup mode just to get their business off the ground. In all honesty I've done that too, though this was before I truly knew how much interest I was paying.

If that's the only way you're going to get make ends meet, if you really do need financing, then do it. However, just understand the risks of what you're doing, and do your best to plan for a rainy day.

PART 3: IN THE MARKETPLACE

THE CUSTOMER PATH AND THE DATING GAME

You wouldn't propose to someone to marry you on the first or second date, would you?

You would get their phone number, take them on a date for coffee or dinner, and as you both become more comfortable with each other, you would progress your relationship appropriately.

Turning a stranger into a customer uses the same logic as dating. You need to progressively increase the relationship at appropriate stages until both parties are ready to commit and your prospect turns into a long-term happy customer.

In order to move a person from stranger to customer, you need to take them along the customer path: from a point where they have never heard about you, your company, your product or your service, and converting them into someone who trusts you enough to give you their money.

It's been said that people want to know, like, trust you before they want to do business with you. That said, less complex products have shorter customer paths and conversely, the more complex your product, and the longer the customer path will be. Your job as a business owner is to walk your customer hand-in-hand along that path.

Another term for the customer path is the sales funnel.

Picture a normal funnel that you would use in your kitchen to pour things into. It's shaped like a V, right?

The way that you pour things into the funnel is similar to the path the customer will take as they begin to know, like and trust you... and eventually do business with you.

As you pour (or place) customers into your funnel, they will move from one stage to the next: Awareness, consideration, decision-making, and finally completing a purchase with you.

You need to make it so that the greatest number of qualified people that enter your funnel come out the other side and as a customer.

To do that, you need to understand:

- What your customers are looking for
- What problems they have
- Why they might be looking at your product or service
- How to provide them with the information and reassurance that they are looking for at each stage

It also helps to know what alternatives your customer has for purchasing so you can compare and contrast the differences and benefits for yourself. (That you'll get from a business plan).

Once you know all of the factors that go into your customer's decision-making process, then you can make the process of buying from you that much easier.

At the top of the funnel is where people are just getting to know who you are.

This is where you will have the greatest number of people entering your funnel. These are people that see your marketing, people that you meet at networking events or trade shows, and people that hear about your business online through social media.

At this point, they are just trying to assess if your company can provide the solution to their problem. All you need to do at this point is to speak to your prospective customer (through your marketing) to say, "Yes, we can help solve your problem. Stick around to learn more."

Once they get to know you and understand that you might be able to solve their problem, they're going to start to like you. They'll start considering you against some of their alternatives.

For your customer, this is a deeper dive into what you can provide for them and if your solution is what they are looking for.

Once the potential customer knows you and likes you, they move through the funnel to a point where they can trust you. They have determined that your product or service meets their needs and are getting closer to parting with their money and giving it to you.

As mentioned earlier, the sales process is different for every company. Your customer could go through your sales funnel and their decision criteria in a few seconds or they could do it in a few years.

If you're selling a simple product like a bottle of water or a commoditized service that people are very familiar with, the customer path is relatively short. If you're selling a very complex product that requires a lot of commitment on the consumer side, then the sales cycle might be quite a bit longer.

It's almost impossible to tell how long your customer path is without measuring it and testing it over time.

As you get more experienced in your business and understand your customer's needs and desires, you can put the pieces in place to shorten the customer path and increase your conversion percentage.

EMAIL LISTS

One of the things that I regret not focusing on earlier in my business was building an email distribution list.

I have a good-sized social media following across multiple platforms, but I don't (at the time of this writing) have a reasonably-sized mailing list that I can use to easily communicate with a targeted audience.

What is an email list?

It's a list of people who have opted in to your email communication.

Why is an email list valuable?

It lets you cut through clutter to communicate directly with your target audience. It allows you to share news, ask for feedback, and promote products that the consumer (the person on your list) has already indicated they want to receive.

While one-on-one communication and individualized emails are more valuable, email distribution lists are more efficient.

Building a list early in your business will help you communicate with the people that want to hear about what you're doing, but might not check your website every week or even every month.

Use the email list to share valuable information with your customers about things they are interested in, as well as news about your business. Grow that list over time, and you'll notice a correlation between sales and traffic increases and the days that your email newsletter goes out.

DON'T MAKE IT HARD ON YOUR CUSTOMERS

I like puns and clever names more than most. However, sometimes they can do more harm than good when it comes to your business.

This chapter is about reducing friction between you and your customer. And when I say friction, I mean an opposing force that exists between you and your customer. Friction can come in many forms, whether that's through your business name, how you pitch your business, how clients get a hold of you, or anything in between.

Getting a new customer is hard enough without extra barriers in the way like a customer not being able to understand what your business is, what you offer or how they can buy from you.

Let's start with your business name.

Does your business name explain clearly what your business does or the customer that it serves? Could someone interpret your business name incorrectly and think you sell something else entirely?

Picking the right business name is critical to early success. Even if you've been in business a long time, it might be worth your while to change your business name if you're getting confusion from the marketplace.

When thinking of a name for your product or your company, go out and do market research to see how it's interpreted before you launch. Cute and clever may make for a good story, but if it doesn't help you sell, is it really a good name for your business?

You know your business better than anyone else. You know what it does, you know why (you think) you're great, and everything is obvious because it's your business.

What about your customer? They are the ones you need to please.

When it comes messaging and explaining why your product is good or better than that of your competitors, you need to address your customer's problems and speak in their language.

Imagine you go traveling to a country that speaks a language that is not your native tongue. You might know a few words, or have a degree of fluency, but there are still barriers to getting the information that you need. Maybe you want directions to a museum or you want to know how much to pay for your meal.

Since you don't speak the language, the interaction is more complicated than it would be with someone who does.

Do you see where I'm going with this?

Speak the language of the person you are doing business with to make your interactions more effective, and ultimately, more successful.

The last tip on reducing friction is making it easy from your customers to buy from you.

Have you ever landed on a website, gone a few clicks and then left because you couldn't find what you were looking for? Have you ever wanted to buy something, but the number of options and pricing were so complicated that you just abandoned it altogether? Or you couldn't find the phone number or the contact details of a place that you knew, so you went to the easier option instead?

I know I have done those things when shopping and I know that people have done that in businesses as well.

The process is never perfect. There will always be friction between your and your prospective customers. You just need to be aware of that friction and take steps: weekly, monthly or whenever is convenient to review your products, your messaging, and your sales process from a customer's point of view and see what you can change to make it easier for them to buy from you.

Reducing friction in your business is much less expensive than adding new customers to your sales pipeline. Reducing friction will pay off in spades if executed properly.

For more on customizing your messaging, look into the concept of A/B testing.

YOUR BUSINESS TALKS BEHIND YOUR BACK

Your reputation precedes you ... and then it speaks about you after you've left.

Everything attached to you, or your business name, speaks to your customers when you aren't around. That includes your website, your business card, and your brand, as well as your reputation and the people you associate with.

In regards to your marketing materials, there's nothing wrong with having business cards that are printed for free, but it's very likely that the person receiving those cards knows that you got them printed for free.

If your website, your cards or your branding look like you've made them yourself, what does that say about your brand and your willingness to invest in yourself?

If you won't invest in yourself, how do you expect your clients to?

Another way that your business can talk about you when you're not around is through social networks like LinkedIn, Facebook and Twitter. They represent an inexpensive way to connect with people, particularly with your target audience that love your product.

The messaging that you share on your branding, your website and your social networks speak to you as a business and as a brand.

It's important to remember that you only control half of your brand; your customer and how they interpret your messages control the other half.

Think of your messaging and your branding from the perspective of your customer and make sure that what you do aligns with your target customer base.

SPOILER ALERT:
RUNNING A BUSINESS IS GOING TO BE HARD

We've all heard the statistics that 80% of businesses fail in the first five years. So statistically, if you start a business, you're more likely going to fail than to succeed.

That might not be the encouraging message that you were looking for in this book, but I didn't want to sugar coat the realities of life as an entrepreneur.

Here are some additional "words of encouragement." There are going to be parts of your business that are going to test you and make your life very challenging. Frankly, parts of it are really going to suck.

I remember in my first business while I was in high school. I was taking meetings at nighttime and choosing to work instead of going out to party or to hang out with my friends. Or coming back from a meeting where someone didn't show up and just wondering if I was doing the right thing, or if I was crazy or stupid.

I find there are three things that can make running a business challenging and if you understand them and can manage your emotions around them, you'll have a much more enjoyable time.

1. You always have something to do.

If you're a new entrepreneur, your list of to-dos will seem endless and daunting. Sometimes, you don't even know where to start or what to do next.

This uncertainty and fear can almost stop you before you even get going. You have things on your mind, keeping you awake at night and often sneaking doubt into your head even when things are going well.

They say the best way to eat an elephant is one bite at a time. So instead of focusing on all the things that you need to do, prioritize and focus on doing one thing at a time. And do them well.

Successful businesses aren't built in a day; they are built day by day, hour by hour and task by task.

Try not to get overwhelmed by all the things you have to do. You'll be way more effective with the things that you do accomplish.

2. Problems never go away.

There will always be something. I have yet to meet an entrepreneur who has smooth sailing all the time. Entrepreneurship is a journey, and there will always be obstacles along the way. They will vary in shape and size, and they will sometimes appear at the worst possible time, but surely as they will come, they will also pass.

I've found that there's no way to get through problems other than to get through them. It seems oversimplified, but you just need to work through a solution and go through the process to get to the other side.

Having a network of other entrepreneurs that you can bounce ideas off of, or who can guide you through this process, is invaluable.

There are times where all my "people" are going through different challenges, and even if it doesn't help my situation per se, it's strangely comforting to know that I'm not "the only one" who goes through these challenges.

Life is challenging and so is entrepreneurship. The ones that achieve success are the ones who are able to overcome their challenges without quitting.

3. Running the business of you isn't easy.

Running a business is challenging, and being a human being has its own challenges too. Balancing family and friends, being a good parent and spouse, and making time for one's personal activities are all tasks that are needed to live a well-balanced life.

Even those that have full time jobs have challenges finding time for everything.

Add to that a new challenge that you've never faced before, that is taking all of your time, a large amount of money, and much of your mental energy, and you're left wondering where you can find the time to add in all that "life stuff."

Add in the fact that entrepreneurs are often faced with social isolation, increased stress, and additional pressure put on by the desire to succeed. How do we as entrepreneurs manage ourselves as well as our businesses?

Everybody has different approaches to balancing their personal and business needs. In my experience and that of others, taking time for meditation, exercise and gratitude top the list. Eating right and sleeping well are also key to longevity. Finally, take the time to sharpen the saw and do things that are not at all related to "work" so that your mind can rest and recover.

Having a morning routine is one of the top tips that I have seen to keep mental and physical performance at its best. Set your day right from the moment you wake up so that you're at your best and ready to conquer whatever life decides to throw at you that day.

If being an entrepreneur were easy, everyone would do it. A life filled with challenges, constant stress, uncertainty and pressure is not for everyone. If you take care of yourself, surround yourself with great people, and approach the journey one step at a time though, you'll be on your way to being a successful entrepreneur.

ADAPT OR DIE

Entrepreneurs are naturally resilient, and as I mentioned earlier, you will learn to be resilient if you're not already.

There are endless studies about what makes a successful entrepreneur and one of the thoughts that tend to come out on top is the ability to go from failure to failure without loss of enthusiasm. I believe this was something that Winston Churchill once said too.

After many failures, you're probably get to a point where you'll find some success in your business. You'll find a secret formula that works best for you.

What I'd encourage you to do is not to get complacent and rely too much on what has worked in the past. Build on that success and continually innovate, change and adapt to the world around you.

The most successful businesses in the world have taken advantage of trends in the marketplace and have rode those waves to great success. If you rest on your past successes for too long, you will miss the boat on next trend and ultimately be left behind. You need to move with the waves.

In order to maintain ahead of the curve, it's important to continually update your business model and, if necessary, change or improve the ways you offer value to your customers. It's an ongoing process and not a one-time adjustment.

Of course, you shouldn't change things up simply for the sake of changing, but rather do it for the sake of adapting to the evolving and shifting needs of your customers. They're not static and you shouldn't be either. Even if you and your business don't change, your customers will move into different stages of their life. Their desires and needs will adapt as a consequence.

Being a customer-focused organization is always a good strategy, but those aren't the only changes that you should consider making.

Technology, tools and process will also evolve over time. Even if your customers or clients aren't demanding these changes, if you're not aware of opportunities for improvement in your business, you might be leaving money on the table. Worse yet, your competitors might use that as an opportunity to take market share from you.

Stay current with business trends and always seek to improve yourself and your business. Not only will it help you stay motivated and passionate about your business, but it will also prove to be a valuable investment.

YOUR BUSINESS MODEL WILL CHANGE OVER TIME

One of my favourite business books is *The Business Model Canvas Playbook*. It's a tool/methodology to build out your business model and how you offer value to your clients.

Your business model has effectively four main parts to it:

1. Operations: What you do in your back office that makes your business run

2. Production: How you make whatever it is that you sell

3. Marketing: How you tell people about your product or service

4. Sales: How you get money from customers

Tasks related to operations and production typically cost money, whereas activities related to marketing and sales typically bring the money in.

Whether or not you've written a formal business plan (you really should have at least a basic business plan), you do have a business model. It's valuable to map out all the aspects of your business model to figure out where there are areas you can improve and where you can offer more value to your customers.

In the previous chapter, we discussed that you have to be ready to adapt to be a successful entrepreneur.

Reviewing, revisiting and revising your business model is a great way to continuously map and monitor potential opportunities to improve your business, as well as to add more value to your business and to create additional profit.

Understanding that you need to adapt and change is the first step in long term success. Taking the time to implement those changes is what comes next.

If you're in the early stages of your business, you'll naturally find opportunities to improve your systems and processes. Regardless of where you are at in your business, though, it's important to take time every week to work on your business and not just in your business.

THE WORST THEY CAN SAY IS NO
(AND YOU'RE GOING TO GET A LOT OF THEM)

As an entrepreneur, you have to wear all of the hats and one of those hats is as a salesperson.

Being is sales in one of the hardest parts of business for a lot of people, because you have to put yourself in a position to get rejected.

There are lots of great sales books out there, so I'm not going to talk about how to get fewer rejections or how to be a more effective salesperson.

What I do want to talk about is the mindset around selling and how you can make the process more enjoyable.

First and foremost, don't let the fear of rejection get in your way. As I mentioned earlier, that's one of the things that still challenges me, but it always gets easier after the first call of the day.

Some of the things that help me get over my fear of rejection are:

- Remembering that they are saying no to my offer, not to me personally.

- Even if they do say "no," that's the worst that can happen. I've never been threatened or yelled at for proposing a deal. (Although I can't speak for everyone.)

- Even a "no" can turn into another opportunity if you ask for a referral.

- Sales are mostly a numbers game. Each time you get a "no," you're getting closer to a "yes."

- If I don't ask the answer is always "no." You miss all the shots you don't take, so just ask.

While not everyone will agree with these tips, these are what have worked for me in the past with my own businesses and my own sales calls.

Keep moving forward. Remember that the reward for a "yes" massively outweighs the hardship of enduring a "no" or two.

F.E.A.R. AND CONCURRING DOUBT

In this book we've talked about having to change, about selling and about the hard skills that you need to be an entrepreneur. One thing that never goes away, even from experienced business people is: FEAR and doubt.

When you're just starting out, FEAR in business and fear of getting out into the world are probably at their highest, but unfortunately it never goes away completely. You just get better at dealing with it, just as you get better at dealing with rejection.

Fear and focus are both muscles that, if properly trained, get stronger and stronger and help you to deal with more complex problems.

First thing to know is that FEAR is not a real thing. It's made up in your mind to stop you from doing things that seem scary.

Disclaimer: If you have fear from doing something stupid or dangerous like playing in a tiger cage, swallowing a sword or anything else that can create bodily harm, I'm not saying that you should ignore what your body is telling you about not doing it.

You might be wondering why I've written FEAR in all caps. That's because FEAR can be described as:

False

Evidence

Appearing

Real

Have you ever noticed that when you imagine a situation in your mind, you almost always create the worst-case scenario? And then, the times that you actually go through with the activity, you usually come back thinking that it wasn't all that bad at all?

Most of the time, that's how fear works.

Your body and your mind create a story to make you think you can't do something because it's scary. Once you conquer yourself and conquer that fear, you realize that you are bigger than the things that were holding you back. You have that power in you.

You're going to be put in many positions where you will doubt yourself. Other people, even some of your closest friends, will doubt you too. What's important to remember is that most of those doubts and fears are man-made. They're not real.

If you go through the business planning process and approach risks sensibly, it should help you address some of your fears and doubts.

There's no magic solution to not being scared or not doubting yourself. It happens to everyone. All you can do is put yourself in a position to be successful. Minimize the risks and uncertainty around you, and surround yourself with people that you can go to when you feel that FEAR and that doubt. They can help talk you through it and help you move past these mental hurdles.

RUNNING A BUSINESS CAN BE LONELY /
SURROUND YOURSELF WITH GOOD PEOPLE

When you decide to run your own business, it's like setting sail towards an island in the middle of the ocean. You can't quite see it, but you think you've got a map. And the only person who knows the destination is you.

You can do your best to share details of your adventure, or why you're going towards this destination, but at the end of the day, you're the only person who sees that vision of where you're going and what you're trying to accomplish.

There have been numerous studies about the effects of being an entrepreneur on the mind and how that type of social isolation turns into depression for many new business owners.

For some, the constant pressure put on by oneself, the social isolation and the stress of running a business each and every day can lead to challenges if you aren't prepared or at least aware of the possible consequences of being an entrepreneur.

Everyone has a different life and family situation. The people around you act as different supports for different things.

In my experience, while family and friends are very helpful in terms of having someone to talk to, unless they understand the particular challenges that you are going through--in your business, in your finances, with your people and your staff--you might just get more frustrated and isolate yourself even further.

To minimize the effects of loneliness and isolation, I recommend building yourself a community of entrepreneurs that you trust and like. This community can be where you can create a safe environment for everyone to share in.

Whether you work with them in collaboration, or just have them to chat with, they will prove invaluable as your move forward and grow your business.

They key is to act as a form of collective intelligence, and not only ask them for help when you need it. You should also be there to listen and support them, as they need it. A rising tide lifts all boats. You can all grow together. These people will become your friends for life and will be there to share in some of your greatest successes.

In the words of an old African proverb:

"If you want to go fast, go alone. If you want to go far, go together."

Find people that you see yourself going far with. It will be one of the best business decisions you will ever make.

PEOPLE BUY FROM PEOPLE, SO GET OUT THERE

You could classify business into one of two types: B to B (or B2B) is business-to-business, whereas B to C (or B2C) is business-to-consumer. Some people might argue that there is really only one type of business: P to P (or P2P), meaning person-to-person.

Whether you have an online business, an offline business or some combination of the two, realize and remember that people buy from people. And the best way to connect with people is to get out there and talk to them.

It can be intimidating, especially for introverts, to build their network and chat with strangers, but an integral part of business is to have conversations with your prospective customers and understand what their needs are so that you can best help them.

There are many technological tools out there to help you connect with people and sell to them, but there is no substitute for having conversations with real human beings, face to face.

Not only does it satisfy our need for personal connections, but also in a practical sense it helps you collect better data and information from your potential customer.

You need to understand your prospect as much as possible, and the more you do, the more successful you'll be in connecting with them and converting them into paying customers.

CONNECT BEFORE YOU PULL

You know the claw machine game in arcades where you can win a stuffed animal by using a claw and successfully capturing it and dropping it in a hole? The challenge is that you have to grab the item just right to be able to win it, because the claw itself is not designed for you to win.

Well, that's very much like building relationships with potential customers.

You need to make sure you fully connect with them before you can "win" them and call them customers or clients.

World famous author and speaker John Maxwell talks about this principle in terms of leadership, and I believe that it's equally applicable with customers and strategic partners.

Would you go to a stranger's house for a party?

Let's say a total stranger walks up to you and invites you to a party at his house. On a scale of 1- 10, how likely are you to go?

Now, let's take that same scenario, except you've seen this person a few times prior and maybe had a few conversations with them. Are you more or less likely to go to the party?

Now, let's say that you and this person have a few mutual friends, you've chatted a few times, and seen each other at many different gatherings with many different people.

Under which of these scenarios would you be mostly likely to end up going to the party? The answer is clear. And the same is true with trying to connect with people for business.

Yes, there will be those times where you hit it off that first time, right out of the blue. But more likely than not, it will take a few interactions, plus a few other factors will need to line up before you connect with that person and you move the relationship forward.

Connect before you pull and you'll have more successful business and personal relationships.

SO WHAT? WHY SHOULD I (THE CUSTOMER) CARE?

Great. So you have a product, company, service or whatever. Why should I, as the customer, care about any of that?

I originally wanted to call this chapter "Your customers don't care about you," because, well... they don't. But I digress.

You'll certainly have customers and other fans and supporters who want to see you succeed, who love your product and who love what you're doing. If you have people like this around you, embrace them, love them, and do everything you can to keep them around. You've certainly earned them.

For the most part though, customers just don't care about you.

Do you know what they care about? Themselves. That's it.

They care about what you can do for them.

They care about how you are going to solve their problem.

They care about getting what your promise them.

They don't care if your car broke down, if your supplier went out of business, or if your staff didn't show up to work today.

You work for them, and that's why they give you their money.

In your marketing, do you talk about yourself or do you talk about your customers?

Do you talk about how good you are or do you talk about what they are going to get from working with you?

Do you talk about how you do what you do or do you talk about how the lives of people you do business with are better because of it?

Your customers don't care about you; they care about themselves. So, when you're marketing, talk about them, not about you, and they'll be far more attentive and much more interested in what you have to say.

DO WHAT YOU DO WELL, AND DO WHAT YOU DO BETTER THAN OTHERS

I'm asked frequently about what kind of business a person should start.

Hopefully, if you're reading this book, you've already begun your path to entrepreneurship. Or maybe you might just be testing the water to figure out what you need to know ahead of time.

Regardless of whether you're a new business owner or you're a soon-to-be new business owner, I recommend building a business that takes advantage of your natural strengths.

What are strengths? Simply put, they are the things that you're good at. It really is that simple.

Moreover, I would also recommend that you start a business that not only uses something that you are good at, but with something you are better at doing than everybody else. This is otherwise known as your competitive advantage.

Building a business on your strengths and competitive advantages is a good idea is because:

1. Starting a business from scratch is hard enough without having to learn how to do the thing that you're trying to sell.

2. Your business is most likely already going to have some level of competition. If you don't enter the market doing something better or different than everyone else, you're going to have an even more challenging time.

Let's say that you have a background as an investment banker. Let's say that you want to open a restaurant. However, you have no past experience with restaurants other than as a diner. And you don't particularly enjoy working in restaurants either. Guess what? You're setting yourself up to have a rather miserable time.

Not only is it going to drain you of your energy, but it's also going to be an expensive learning experience.

It's been said that strengths are what give you energy and weaknesses are what drain energy from you.

Keeping in mind that building a business is one of the hardest things you will ever do, do you want to be building a business on something that takes energy away from you or something that gives you energy?

Build off your strengths when building or growing a business and use those strengths and competitive advantages to create a profitable and successful business.

UNTIL YOU HAVE THE CHEQUE, THERE IS NO DEAL

I know it's easy to get excited about someone (anyone) to show interest in your product or service, and then to make plans for what you're going to do with that cheque and work from there.

I've had lots of those experiences:

"Oh yeah, this deal is in the bag."

" Yeah, we're pretty much done."

"Totally a new client! This is going to be amazing."

If you haven't experienced this yet or you still believe that when a customer comes to you promising that they'll be a new client and you start providing services for them assuming that everything is going to be fine, I'll let you in on a little secret: if they don't pay, they're not a client.

You save yourself lots of time by understanding that clients or potential clients just want things for free a lot of the time and you're inclined to give it to them, because you want them to be a client or customer. Realize that unless they pay you for something, they're not a customer. The deal is not done until you get the cheque.

I've had dozens of "certain" deals that felt like they were 100% in the bag, only to see them fall apart before getting that cheque.

The reason I share this with you is because you'll save yourself a lot of time and money not bending over backwards for these soon-to-be (but not quite there yet) clients and not starting any work for them until they pay you.

MOST PEOPLE AREN'T READY TO BUY FROM YOU WHEN YOU FIRST MEET THEM

I've heard that only three percent of a market is actively looking to buy what you sell at any given time. Another 30 percent has a need, but isn't ready to act right away. The rest of the market doesn't need what you have or even know who you are.

Considering that a majority of the time the people you market to don't want what you have to offer right now, what does that mean for your business and your marketing?

This means that people fall into one of two groups. One group of people will never want what you are selling, so they aren't even your customers. That's great, because it means that you won't waste your time marketing to them. The other group of people might be the ones you've just met and can be a customer. You just need to spend the time earning their trust, getting them to like you and your company, and waiting for the time when they are actually ready to buy.

One thing that I've had to learn is that you can't make anyone buy anything. At the same time, a good salesperson keeps in communication with that person and is available for them when they are eventually ready to buy.

According to a study of sales habits:

- 2% of sales are made on the first contact
- 3% of sales are made on the second contact
- 5% of sales are made on the third contact
- 10% of sales are made on the fourth contact
- 80% of sales are made on the fifth to twelfth contact

There are a few reasons why that might be.

Either the potential customer just couldn't stand to be bothered by the salesperson any longer and just caved or, the more likely option, is that the salesperson was able to determine the customer's needs in the earlier cases and was able to stay in touch over that time so that when the prospect was ready to buy, the salesperson was there, ready to take the order.

Understanding the customer process, and understanding that most customers aren't going to buy from you right away is critical to understanding the long-term viability and success of your business.

Being able to market to them over time using Email lists and other tools will help keep your company top of mind so that when the customer is ready to buy they come to you.

NOTHING HAPPENS WITHOUT THE SALE

› PART 1: DON'T GIVE AWAY YOUR BUSINESS

Everyone has different motivations for going into business. Some just want a way to make money, some want freedom, and some want to help people, among thousands of other possibilities.

I believe that most successful entrepreneurs aren't driven by money. Rather they are driven by the opportunity to help people, to offer services and products that are going to help make people's lives better.

Especially in the early stages of business, you just want to get your product into the hands of people, letting them know how you can help them and offer your services. What's important to remember is that you're in business to sell things, and nothing in your business moves forward without the sale.

You might really be able to help people with what you offer, but if no one is willing and able to pay for it, then do you have a good business?

I know what you're thinking, because I've thought it too: "If I give my product away and let people try it, then they will come back and buy it."

Sometimes that's true, but I'll tell you that I've spent more money than I care to admit on samples, trials and promotional materials when I should have been focusing my energy (and money) on targeting the best clients for my products. I should have been focusing on the potential clients who had the budget to pay for what I was selling. I should have been marketing to the people who were actually going to buy products like the ones I offered.

When you write your business plan, or create your strategy on how to get customers, one of the things that will help you the most is figuring out who your customers are. And perhaps even more importantly, you'll want to figure out who your customers aren't.

If you do that early in the game, you'll avoid wasting money on those non-customers, and focus your time and energy on the ones that are most likely to buy.

> PART **2**: MANAGING YOUR TIME INTO SELLING AND BUILDING ACTIVITIES

You only have so much time in the day, and even if you have employees, you need to manage your own time into where it will produce the best returns in the business.

There are effectively two ways you can spend your time:

1. Working on improving your business systems, processes and products

2. Selling and marketing your business

The challenge lies in the fact that there is no perfect way to manage your time. Also realize that your needs and the needs of your business will shift as time goes on.

During the startup stage, you'll need to spend much of your time developing your systems and product, and then taking that to the market of potential customers to see how they feel about what you have and if they are willing to pay for it. You then go back into your laboratory (your home, office, or wherever you work from) to refine your product and repeat the cycle.

Depending on how sophisticated your product is, you may need to put in more work on product development.

If your product literally "sells itself," then you've done a great job matching it to your customer and you've done a great job building an effective system for delivering it.

CUSTOMER PROFILES: WHO IS YOUR CUSTOMER?

One of the worst mistakes you can make as a new business owner is saying that everyone is your customer.

Even products that everyone uses (laundry detergent, toilet paper, toothpaste, and so on) have their own customer profiles. Different people buy them for different reasons. One group might want one type of detergent, while another group will desire an entirely different set of benefits.

The reason it is so important to specify who buys your product is because you need to "speak" to these people directly as part of your selling and marketing process. When I say "speak," I mean communicate in a way that shows you understand who they are, what their life is like, and what they value as part of their everyday or professional lives.

Think of it as if you were in a different country, trying to communicate with the local people. If you don't "speak their language," you aren't going to get anywhere.

The more you understand your customer, the more effectively you can speak their language and the more effective you can be in your marketing and communications.

What does effective mean? It means you'll have higher engagement, higher closing rates, and higher ROI on your marketing.

There's one more benefit to understanding who your customer is: you'll stop wasting money on ineffective marketing.

I use the analogy of TV channels, but it truly does cross over with different marketing channels.

Have you ever noticed that the commercials on the sports channel or on the food channel are different than the ones on the kids channel or for when you're watching the news or the weather?

That's because the people putting those ads out know who their customers are and where they hang out. In other words, they know where they can reach them. They don't bother spending money on (marketing) channels where they won't find their customers. As a business owner, you need to do the same thing.

Once you determine who your best customers are, you can figure out where they live and where they spend their time. That way, you can stop wasting money on channels that don't work for you.

(Visit elevatedbusinesslife.com for a marketing strategy template with over 100 different marketing channels to start developing your approach.)

THE ART OF THE PITCH (ELEVATOR OR OTHERWISE)

Throughout the chapters of this book, we've been discussing how to reach your customers, how to add value as part of your business model, how to help the right people, and how to market and sell yourself.

This is one of the most important (and most fun) chapters of the book.

This is where you learn how to make a great pitch.

Most people have heard the term "elevator pitch." The term is derived from when people used to talk to each other in elevators, before the era where people had their earphones in or stared at their phones until their destination.

If you do happen to walk into an elevator with someone and they are engaged in a conversation with you, you're in luck. In fact, an effective "elevator pitch" is useful in any situation where you have a small window of time to tell people about your business, product or service.

I find that most people tune out around 8 seconds in if they aren't interested. You can probably get to the full 30 seconds if you have caught their attention and you have something interesting to share.

One final note before we get into the how, whether you want to believe me or not: There is no escaping pitching your business. It's everywhere. Whether you network or not (you should network), invariably people will ask you, "So, what do you do?"

Whether they actually care, or are just making conversation, you should be prepared to answer the question intelligibly and in a way that makes what you do sound interesting. Who knows? They might know someone who could be a customer, a strategic partner, or an investor.

Some of the most interesting relationships and opportunities I've ever had have come out of networking, so don't discount it.

The other type of pitching, really pitching, comes when you're in a room of people trying to promote your product, look for investors or share your story.

A good elevator pitch combines many of the chapters of this book into a short story about your business.

Here are the points you need to cover in order:

- Your business name
- What problem does it solve
- For what specific customer
- By doing what?
- How is it different than other similar solutions out there

Your pitch will change, adapt and evolve over time, because otherwise you'll sound like a robot. What I find is the most valuable part of the pitch is explaining what you do differently or what makes you unique.

If there's nothing new or different about your business, your product or service, then you're going to have a hard time getting attention with your marketing. But if you can find what makes you different or better, you're going to get more attention and more dollars from customers too.

(For a video on how to nail the pitch visit elevatedbusinesslife.com)

YOU HAVE TO BE FIRST, BETTER OR DIFFERENT

This is one of the most interesting anecdotes on business value creation that I've heard in a very long time. I was at a networking event and one of the speakers stated it ever so simply.

"For you to be successful in your business, you need to be first, better or different."

What does that actually mean?

Look at businesses involved in innovation and technology. To be successful, they oftentimes have to be the first in the market.

Earlier in the book, we talked about ideas being a dime a dozen. There are certainly a lot of great ideas out there, but it's the person or business who acts on those ideas first who become successful.

Let's say that you didn't come up with the idea before anyone else. Don't worry. You still have hope if you can be the best in your business. Recognize this. You have to be remarkably fortunate and lucky to be first. Even if you're not first, you can always become the best. If the guy who was first has an inferior solution, you'll still win.

But what if you're neither first nor are you the best? Where does that leave you?

We can always be different. The truth is that most businesses are neither first nor the best. You're not reinventing the wheel and with thousands of companies doing the same thing, being the absolute best is overwhelmingly difficult. This means that the rest of us are left to compete with one another. What does being different really mean?

It means offering different services and different value. It means aligning your product or service with who you are as a person and who you are as a business.

As mentioned earlier, building on what you do well (your strengths) and what you do better than anyone else (your competitive advantage) is going to help you create that differentiation in a way that separates you from your competitors.

That's precisely why you want to be different. When you stack up against your competitors, when you are compared, you want to offer something that will resonate with people. You want them to move closer to you, not further away. The worst thing that could happen is indifference and the perception that you are exactly the same as everybody else.

Dare to be different. Dare to elicit that response.
Dare people to care.

SOMETIMES YOU DON'T NEED TO BE THE BEST, JUST THE BEST-KNOWN

Marketing is funny. People are funny. Put the two together and you never know what is going to happen.

We've talked about creating value, sharing what makes you great, speaking to your customers directly and doing what you can to be the best. Sometimes, though, you don't need to have any of those things; you just need to be in the right place at the right time and stay there.

One of the key factors defining success in marketing and advertising is whether or not people can recall the name of the company that they just saw in an advertisement. It doesn't matter how memorable, how clever, how insightful or how funny your ad might be if people can't associate the advertisement with your company. Otherwise, it's just some entertainment that gets lost in the ether.

Far more important than being able to remember the advertisement itself is your customer's ability to recall the name of your company when they happen to be in the market for one of the products that you sell. This is crucially important even if their initial inclination isn't even to buy from you necessarily. They just want to buy a product like the one you have. Or perhaps they want to refer someone who has that need to a solution.

If the name of your company is front of mind for your niche, industry or product class, then it's going to be the first name that pops into the heads of your potential customers. They'll think of you before they think of your competitors, even if you don't necessarily have the "best" solution or offer the "best" value.

People like familiarity. Seeing and recognizing a name that they already know provides a sense of comfort and along with this comes with some sense of trustworthiness. They're far more likely to go with brands and products that they know than risk going with some brand they've never heard of before.

This is one of the reasons that it's hard to get people to switch from their favourite brands. Your product could be better or cheaper or even free, but if the competing brand has strong customer loyalty, you will really struggle with getting that customer to buy from you instead. The "other" brand that they're already using is too comfortable, too familiar.

The good news is that you can also leverage this phenomenon in your favour by building up that familiarity and brand loyalty with your own customers and your own company.

Use advertising and marketing where the primary goal is to keep your company or brand "top of mind" with their customers. This way, when they think about a service provider or company to provide a solution to their problem, yours is the name that comes first.

This strategy goes hand-in-hand with relationship building. No amount of advertising will help you if your product is sub-par.

There are many ways that you can stay top of mind for your customer through advertising:

- Monthly or quarterly email newsletters discussing common problems people might have (and how you help them)
- Coupons and promos in the mail
- In-person meetings
- Frequent social media posts
- Trade shows in the community
- Sponsoring events
- Fridge magnets
- Billboards and car-wrap advertising

For a more exhaustive list see the marketing menu at elevatedbusinesslife.com

If you're going to employ marketing to develop brand awareness and foster brand loyalty, ensure that you have a pitch or specific offering that can be associated with your brand and your company only.

People should know exactly what they should turn to your business to get. If you're selling both hair extensions and fireworks (Random example I know), customers will only get confused. They don't know why you're the expert in either, so they'll assume that you're the expert in neither.

Part of effective marketing is creating a key promise or expectation to establish you as the go to source for what they are looking for.

Some famous promises in marketing have helped companies achieve that invaluable mind space from their customers.

Dominos: 30 minutes or less or it's free

Avis: We're second, so we try harder

Fedex: When it absolutely, positively needs to get there overnight

These are just company slogans with the brand promise in them, but for many years, they served as a cue for the customer when they were looking for that type of service. Some might seem corny and cheesy, like some jingles that you might be able to recall, but if you remember it, that means that it worked.

You might not be able to be the best, but you can always work to be the best-known.

Stand on your own brand promise. Use whatever method makes the most sense for you to gain the mindshare (and wallet share) from your target customer.

Offer something remarkable and notable and you'll get better return on investment (ROI) on your marketing.

COMPETITION FOR YOUR BENEFIT

When you come up with a brand new product or service, coming up with something that the marketplace has never seen before, you might think that you don't have any competition. You might think that because you're a new business or because what you're doing is so revolutionary, you don't have any competition.

I'm sorry to tell you, but every business has competition. Even yours, no matter how novel or unique you might think it is.

This may not be in the form of direct competition in terms of other companies trying to take business away from you. Rather, it could be in the form of alternatives for your customer.

It's not about the product or service itself as much as it is about what the customer is looking for the product to do.

Your product or service has a benefit to it. There's a reason why people are willing to pay for it. It's because they are getting something in return: value.

We've discussed this notion a little earlier on in the book. Maybe you're the only company making widgets, but if another company makes sprockets and a customer might choose a sprocket over a widget, you've got competition.

Think, before you came along, how were people getting that value in their lives? How were they getting the desired benefit? How were they solving the problem that your product or service is seeking to address?

Imagine that you are Alexander Graham Bell. Imagine that you're trying to sell the world's first telephone. There are no other telephones at this point, so you think that you're sitting pretty. After all, you have no competition, right?

Not exactly.

Before the modern telephone came into existence, people had

other ways to get in touch with one another. They could meet up in person and talk face to face. They could send telegrams to one another. They could send letters through the postal service. They could communicate with Morse code. They had, and continue to have options.

You are selling communication. You are not selling a "telephone," per se.

Going back to the present day, whatever you think you are selling, your customer has alternatives for how they are going to get that benefit already.

It doesn't matter what sort of business you're in and what sort of product you sell. Maybe your customer could simply buy a different product from a different company. Maybe the solution is just to do nothing, because that's more desirable than paying for what you have to offer.

If you want to get traction with your business, look at the benefits of your products, and look at other places where your customer can get those benefits. That's your competition. Now go out there and be better than the alternatives.

SELLING SOMETHING MEANS CHANGING BEHAVIOR

This is something that took me a very long time to learn and to incorporate into my business.

You might have a great idea for a product or service. You might have a great platform to get it to people. The challenge is that people have their routines. They have what they're used to doing. And getting people to change their routine to integrate your product or service is going to be one of the hardest things you will ever do in business.

More often than not, your product, no matter how simple or amazing it might be, will require some sort of change on the customer's behalf. It might mean changing where they are currently buying a particular type of product. It might mean changing the process they are already using or incorporating a whole new type of behavior that is completely foreign to them.

There are a lot of people who come up with apps and technology products where new users might try it once or twice. However, after that brief honeymoon period, these users don't really incorporate these apps and technology products in their lives on a long-term basis. So, they just go back to what they were doing before.

Creating a great product is the first step, getting someone to try it is the next step, but if you want to have long term success, ensure that people incorporate your product into their daily lives.

You might have to need to remind your customer frequently about your product so that it becomes a cornerstone of their everyday life. These reminders can come in the form of emails, personal messages, advertising, or any other method that you use to communicate with them. The key is to communicate these messages in a helpful tone so as to not bother the person; you want them to enjoy using your product, not make it feel like a chore or an extra thing to add on.

Changing behavior and adding opportunities for use will help you retain more customers for longer periods of time and will ultimately determine the successful adoption of your product or service.

THE TRADE-OFF OF COST VERSUS QUALITY

Good, fast and cheap: You can only choose two.

This is the universal rule if you need anything in your life. If you're looking at hiring a service provider, or if you are a service provider yourself, this is a good rule to follow.

Want something good and fast? It's going to cost you.

Want something fast and cheap? It might not be that good.

Want something good and cheap (or even free)? It's probably going to take a while.

In other words, you get what you pay for (most of the time).

Let's say that you have a cousin who can design a website for you for free. That sounds like a pretty good deal, but you might be waiting on changes and updates for far longer than you want. You're paying for this "free" website with your time and patience.

Let's say that you have some graphic design work that you need to get done, like creating new business cards or a media kit. Let's say that you want this job to be done quickly and you want it to be of high quality. That's great, except you can probably expect to pay a premium for that. You're paying, literally, with your money.

Let's say that you want to have a full yet inexpensive meal prepared for you in under a minute. Don't be surprised if this meal is nowhere near the same quality that you might be able to enjoy if the food was cooked fresh instead. That would take more time.

It's all one big trade-off and that's something you're going to have to accept both as a service provider and as a customer of service providers. If you are trying to offer all three of these core values to your customer all at once -- low cost, high quality, and fast delivery -- you're going to do at least one of them poorly.

Instead, it is a far superior strategy to focus on delivering just one or two of these promises consistently. That's far smarter and more successful in the long run than fluctuating your offering. Be consistent in what to offer. If you're going to be good and fast, charge a premium. If you're going to be cheap and good, don't promise the fastest service.

And even when you are purchasing products or paying for services for your own business, keep this rule in mind. Remember that you get what you pay for, since no one can offer good, fast and cheap all at the same time on a consistent basis. Be prepared to shell out a few extra bucks on the things that matter most, as in most cases, it's going to be worth it in the long run.

IT'S (PROBABLY) NOT GOING TO GO AS QUICKLY AS YOU WOULD HAVE WANTED

I'd caution you from getting into the elevator business; It's really up and down...

(I wasn't going to write a book without at least one pun in it.)

We've chatted about the different challenges that you have to overcome to be an entrepreneur. We've talked about developing hard skills, soft skills and the right mindset, but there's one thing that I can't prepare you for: the journey.

There are lots of pictures out there about how the life of an entrepreneur resembles a roller coaster ride, that the path to success has many twists and turns, and that growth in a business is typically accompanied by first taking a step backwards.

There's nothing that can prepare you for your journey. Parts of it are going to be amazing, parts of it are going to be infuriating, and some parts are going to outright suck. That's the honest truth. These are the tradeoffs, however, for doing something amazing and building something for yourself and for your future.

One of my favourites quotes is:

"Ride the spiral to the end. You may just go where no one's been." - Tool

Your entrepreneurial journey is uniquely yours and I have no idea what the future holds for you when you put this book down. All I can do is let you know that things might not go as fast as you'd like or as fast as you might expect.

There are certainly many companies that have experienced rocket ship growth and have achieved tremendous success in short amounts of time. I'm sure you could be one of them. Could be.

I would say those companies are the exceptions, and not the

rule. Even some of the "overnight successes" that you see on tech blogs around the Internet or on the cover of business magazines have been slogging away for years before they found the recipe for what worked for them. It did not happen overnight.

Do your best to plan, move quickly, execute, get it done and then see what happens. It might not go the way you planned. Or it might go ten times faster than your wildest dreams. Anything is possible.

No matter the pace your business goes now or in the future, I'll be the first person to congratulate you for taking the leap, making moves and chasing your dream.

Which leads me to my last piece of advice...

ALL YOU HAVE TO DO IS START (AND KEEP GOING)

I've always believed that the fear of regret is worse than the fear of failure.

My greatest fear is lying on my deathbed and meeting the person that I could have been. I would rather fail hard on my journey than to live wondering what I could have created, what I could have done, what impact I could have had on the world.

Whether you're well into your path of entrepreneurship already or you're looking at starting a business, my best advice to you is to take a calculated risk and just go for it.

Beyond the benefits of financial gain, freedom of time and overall greater life fulfilment, creating a business is going to have an immeasurable impact on your community, your staff, and your customers. And you.

Not all businesses are winners. You may lose money or you may decide that the life of an entrepreneur is not for you. Let's be real; it's not for everyone. If history has taught us anything, it's that those who dare, those who risk failure, those who take the leap to make something great are the ones who have made life better for all of humanity.

The world's greatest inventions, vaccines, and advances in technology have come from people who decided to take the leap of faith, to do something that they had never done before, in an effort to impact the world in the way they never imagined possible.

You might be thinking, "But Anthony, I'm just starting a small business selling X. I'm not trying to change the world."

Every big business started off as just a startup. Even if you don't want to build a huge business, just a way to replace your job, make some extra money on the side, or do something that fuels your creative side, you owe it to yourself to take the leap and make it happen.

There is no one path to success. It's whichever path you take and you continue on until you reach your destination. Who knows? You may just go where no one's ever been.

To your success!

OTHER FAQS

Should I incorporate?

There are two main reasons why someone would incorporate their business: Legal protection and tax benefits.

First, consult with an accountant and lawyer to see if it's right for your specific situation. Being incorporated will result in a significantly higher cost to doing your taxes, as well as increased legal costs on a yearly basis.

The benefits are that you will be taxed at a corporate rate (probably lower than your personal income) and that if someone wants to sue you, they sue the corporate entity (i.e., your corporation) and not you as the individual.

What social networks should I be using? Do I need to be on all of them?

Go back to the chapter about marketing channels and think about where your customer "lives" on the Internet.

You might not be a social media expert, but having a business profile on LinkedIn, Facebook and Twitter should be your basic necessities in this day and age. They will complement your web presence and they are channels to allow you to communicate with potential customers who might not know about your business yet.

What's the best software for a small business?

The best software is the one that works for you, and the one that saves your time, money and energy.

There are lots of different types of software that can help you with your:

- Accounting
- Customer relationship management
- Social media
- Email Marketing
- Project management
- Internal communication
- And more

Every day, there are new programs and solutions getting released. Some are the most commonly used, but that doesn't mean that they are necessarily the best solution for you.

For a list of business software that I recommend, visit www.elevatedbusinesslife.com/small-business-software

To ask your own questions and to see other people's questions visit: elevatedbusinesslife.com

Sales funnel

The sales funnel is the process in which a person first learns about your services, becomes interested in your services, becomes a lead, and then finally, a customer or client

Leading and lagging indicators

A leading indicator is an indicator of an event that will occur in the future and is usually prediction or statistic based. This gives a hint BEFORE a new trend or major event.

Lagging indicators

A lagging indicator is an aspect of the business that changes after an event has happened.

Unique value proposition

This statement should set you apart from competitors. A unique value (or sales) proposition defines what you do best, how you can solve your target market's needs, and what the clear benefits to your service are. This is a very important aspect of a business plan and a marketing campaign.

Customer lifetime value

The customer lifetime value is an estimate of what a customer will spend with your company over time, rather than through an individual purchase.

Pitch decks

A pitch deck is a very quick or brief presentation or demonstration that showcases your product or service and business plan. This is usually to show to investors, outside help (management consultants), partners, customers, or anyone with potential interest in your business.

A/B Testing

A/B testing is making slight variations on text, imagery, and other pieces of content and measuring which ones perform better. Version A might have a 10% conversion rate where as option B had a 50% conversion rate.

Elevator pitch

An elevator pitch is a short speech about who you are and what you offer. Hence the name, it should take the length of an elevator ride to deliver. This speech should be well prepared, clear and concise.

SEO

Search Engine Optimization is a tool to help create more visibility for your website through search results. Contributing factors to SEO are keywords, outside links, internal links, photo titles, regular blog posts and page titles

Writing content on your website with relevant keywords that match search terms will help prospective customers find your website.

AdWords:

AdWords is a google online advertising service. AdWords picks up on keywords from your website and when searched, may display content from your site with a link to the specific page

Conversion:

Conversion is the rate in which site visitors and leads turn into customers. This can be quantified through various online services. Conversion is measured by a conversion rate formula, which is fairly simple: The number of paying customers divided by the total website visitors will give you the percentage of conversion. Conversion closely ties in with funnel marketing, SEO and other concepts important to both offline and online marketing.

Lead magnet

A lead magnet is an incentive to attract your target market. Examples: free downloads, limited time sales, or other offers that will bring them to your site and require them to provide some information about themselves, such as name, Email address, employer, or other relevant information.

Email newsletter

An Email newsletter is an online communication and marketing tool used to communicate with current customers & clients, as well as prospective clients and leads. Email newsletters are best if sent fairly regularly, ie: on a quarterly, monthly, or bi-weekly basis. Newsletters should offer new and interesting information, but also be concise. An ideal message open rate is around 20-25% (or more!).

Bootstrapping

In reference to business, bootstrapping is a start up term for a business opening up with no outside help or funding. The term can be applied to other areas, such as marketing, or any area in life that requires creative thinking and ingenuity in place of external funding.

Web hosting

Web hosts provide server space so that your website can be accessible to the public via "www". An example of a web host is Go Daddy. Some web hosts also sell domain names and offer platform services to build sites on.

Within web hosting, there are a variety of types of hosting which can affect the overall speed of loading for your site. Free & shared hosting will often be slow and could crash with a high amount of traffic. Paid hosting is usually on a scale, determined by estimated traffic to your site. A large corporate site will be more expensive to host than a personal web page or blog.

RSS:

RSS is a web feed (can be translated to Rich Site Summary, or Really Simple Syndication). An RSS feed allows people to subscribe to a service where content is regularly created. They will receive a notification from the content creator each time a new item is published. Blogs, audio, and video. RSS feeds are great for fast changing content.

Burn Rate

As your business grows you will have time where you are spending more money than you are making. Your burn rate is the monthly excess in costs over revenue.

Runway

Your runway is how much money or time you have left before you spend you spend all your money. Like a plane has so much runway before it takes off, you company needs to take off before you run out of money.

ROI

Return on investment refers to a ratio used to measure the benefits of an investment. ROI ends up being the ratio from all gains and income subtracted by all costs including and after the initial investment. Depending on the business size, there are complicated and less complicated ways of calculating this number. The smaller the business, the less complicated it is to gather the return on investment.

Vision

Your vision is an important part of your business planning process where you predetermine where you would like you business to be in the future. By creating a vision for your company it gives you a desired end point for your company in the future.

For more business terms visit: elevatedbusinesslife.com

BOOK RECOMMENDATIONS

The Business Model Canvas Playbook by Marco Meyer

The E-myth Revisited by Michael E. Gerber

Built to Sell by John Warrillow and Bo Burlingham

Scarcity by Sendhil Mullainathan and Eldar Shafir

The 21 Irrefutable Laws of Leadership by John C. Maxwell and Steven R. Covey

Getting Things Done: The Art of Stress-Free Productivity by David Allen and James Fallows

The Art of War by Sun Tzu

Selling the Invisible by Harry Beckwith (For a service business)

For more book recommendations visit: elevatedbusinesslife.com

Online Bonuses:

- Marketing template
- E-book on strategic planning
- List of online software
- Video presentation on core competencies.
- Balanced scorecard

Visit www.elevatedbusinesslife.com to download these tools.

Made in the USA
San Bernardino, CA
22 June 2018